Rich States, Poor States

ALEC-Laffer State Economic Competitiveness Index

Arthur B. Laffer

Stephen Moore

Jonathan Williams

$\mathcal{A}$LEC

AMERICAN LEGISLATIVE EXCHANGE COUNCIL

Rich States, Poor States
ALEC-Laffer State Economic Competitiveness Index
© 2011 American Legislative Exchange Council

Published by
American Legislative Exchange Council
1101 Vermont Ave., NW, 11th Floor
Washington, D.C. 20005

Phone: (202) 466-3800
Fax: (202) 466-3801

www.alec.org

Dr. Arthur B. Laffer, Stephen Moore
and Jonathan Williams, Authors

Designed by Drop Cap Design | www.dropcapdesign.com

ISBN: 978-0-9822315-8-6

Rich States, Poor States: ALEC-Laffer State Economic Competitiveness Index has been published by the American Legislative Exchange Council (ALEC) as part of its mission to discuss, develop, and disseminate public policies, which expand free markets, promote economic growth, limit the size of government, and preserve individual liberty. ALEC is the nation's largest nonpartisan, voluntary membership organization of state legislators, with 2,000 members across the nation. ALEC is governed by a Board of Directors of state legislators, which is advised by a Private Enterprise Board representing major corporate and foundation sponsors.

ALEC is classified by the Internal Revenue Service as a 501(c)(3) nonprofit and public policy and educational organization. Individuals, philanthropic foundations, corporations, companies, or associations are eligible to support ALEC's work through tax-deductible gifts.

Table of Contents

About the Authors

DR. ARTHUR B. LAFFER

Arthur B. Laffer is the founder and chairman of Laffer Associates, an economic research and consulting firm, as well as Laffer Investments, an institutional investment firm. As a result of Laffer's economic insight and influence in starting a worldwide tax-cutting movement during the 1980s, many publications have named him "The Father of Supply-Side Economics." He is a founding member of the Congressional Policy Advisory Board, which assisted in forming legislation for the 105th, 106th and 107th Congresses. Laffer served as a member of President Reagan's Economic Policy Advisory Board for both terms. In March 1999, he was noted by *Time Magazine* as one of "the Century's Greatest Minds" for his invention of the Laffer Curve, which has been called one of "a few of the advances that powered this extraordinary century." He has received many awards for his economic research, including two Graham and Dodd Awards from the Financial Analyst Federation. He graduated from Yale with a Bachelor's degree in economics in 1963 and received both his MBA and Ph.D. in economics from Stanford University.

STEPHEN MOORE

Stephen Moore joined *The Wall Street Journal* as a member of the editorial board and senior economics writer on May 31, 2005. He splits his time between Washington, D.C., and New York, focusing on economic issues including budget, tax, and monetary policy. Moore was previously the founder and president of the Club for Growth, which raises money for political candidates who favor free-market economic policies. Over the years, Moore has served as a senior economist at the Congressional Joint Economic Committee, as a budget expert for The Heritage Foundation, and as a senior economics fellow at the Cato Institute, where he published dozens of studies on federal and state fiscal policy. He was also a consultant to the National Economic Commission in 1987 and research director for President Reagan's Commission on Privatization.

JONATHAN WILLIAMS

Jonathan Williams is the director of the Tax and Fiscal Policy Task Force for the American Legislative Exchange Council (ALEC), where he works with state legislators, Congressional leaders, and members of the private sector to develop free-market fiscal policy solutions for the states. Prior to joining ALEC, Williams served as staff economist at the non-partisan Tax Foundation, authoring numerous tax policy studies. His research on gasoline taxes was featured by the Congressional National Surface Transportation Infrastructure Financing Commission.

Williams's work has appeared in many publications including *The Wall Street Journal*, *The Los Angeles Times*, *Forbes,* and *Investor's Business Daily.* He has been a contributing author to the Reason Foundation's Annual Privatization Report and has written for the Ash Center for Democratic Governance and Innovation at Harvard's Kennedy School of Government. In addition, Williams is a contributing author of "In Defense of Capitalism" (Northwood University Press, 2010). He is also a contributor to *The*

Examiner (Washington, D.C.) and serves as an adjunct fiscal policy fellow at the Kansas Policy Institute. In addition to testifying before numerous legislative bodies and speaking to audiences across America, Williams is a frequent guest on talk radio shows and has appeared on numerous television outlets, including the PBS NewsHour with Jim Lehrer and *Fox Business News.*

A Mid-Michigan native, Williams graduated magna cum laude from Northwood University in Midland, Mich., majoring in economics, banking/finance, and business management. While at Northwood, he was the recipient of the prestigious Ludwig von Mises Award in Economics.

Acknowledgements

We wish to thank the following parties for making this publication possible:

First, our sincere thanks go to the Searle Freedom Trust and the Claude R. Lambe Charitable Foundation for their generous support of this research.

Next, we thank Ron Scheberle, Michael Bowman, Chaz Cirame, Rob Shrum, Laura Elliott, Kati Siconolfi, Greg Phelps, Victoria Andrew, Meaghan Archer, Theodore Lafferty, and the professional staff of ALEC for their assistance in publishing this in a timely manner. We also appreciate the research assistance of Tyler Grimm, Ford Scudder, Mark Wise, Scott Vaughn, Ken Petersen, and Wayne Winegarden. We hope these research findings help lead to the enactment of pro-growth economic policies in all 50 state capitals.

Foreword

Dear ALEC Member,

Rich States, Poor States should be required reading for governors, legislators, and those who serve them. Money is spent more efficiently by the private sector than by governments, so it is reasonable to expect that states with lower overall taxes have better economic environments than states with high taxes and more government spending. It is true that lowering taxes can be politically difficult: even fiscal conservatives start losing their enthusiasm for cutting taxes when special interest groups that consume a state's tax dollars warn them that tax cuts will have dire consequences. But the consequences of being caught in a spiral of increased taxes and a decreasing rate of return on the tax base are much more dangerous. Arthur Laffer, Stephen Moore, and Jonathan Williams use a clear, concise format to expose the scare tactics of the tax-and-spend crowd and show how economic vitality follows lower taxes.

It is true that the policies of the federal government have a direct effect on the economic environment of the entire country, but governors and legislatures are not rudderless. We can and must start to change our country's economic course by providing an environment that rewards our citizens for their efforts and their risks. The founders of our country understood that a republic with its multiple states was the perfect incubator for vetting competing approaches to public policies. *Rich States, Poor States* illustrates the outcomes of various tax policies at the state level throughout the country. The evidence is overwhelming and the proper course is clear: States should pursue policies that leave more money in our citizens' pockets to help fuel and drive our economy.

I'd like to thank the authors for their contribution to the effort to restore economic prosperity to our great country. To those who doubt their research, I encourage you to watch Kansas during the next few years as we work to reset the state's course on taxes and let our citizens once again be the engine of economic growth.

Sincerely,

Sam Brownback

Sam Brownback
Governor of Kansas

Executive Summary

Bloated state spending levels and trillions of dollars in unfunded government employee pension liabilities pose huge financial obstacles to economic recovery in the 50 states today. This begs the million—or trillion—dollar question: Why are some states prospering while others are still struggling?

In this fourth edition of *Rich States, Poor States*, Arthur B. Laffer, Stephen Moore, and Jonathan Williams discuss the best practices to enable states to drive economic growth, create jobs, and improve the standard of living for their citizens. The authors also provide the 2011 ALEC-Laffer State Economic Competitiveness Index of the states, based on states' economic policies. Through the empirical evidence and analysis contained within these pages, discover which policies lead to state economic growth and which policies states should avoid.

In chapter 1, the authors examine the states' fiscal conditions and discuss the new possibilities for future fiscal reforms. This chapter focuses on this year's top performing states and those that continue to struggle. Data from the latest U.S. census demonstrates that taxpayers continue to vote with their feet by moving to states with more competitive business climates. The evidence from population changes over the past decade speaks for itself. According to the 2010 census, the nine states without personal income taxes, which accounted for only 19 percent of the overall population at the start of the decade, experienced 35 percent of all population growth in America. This chapter also outlines key threats to states' financial health, including unsustainable government pension plans and other anti-growth policies.

Chapter 2 surveys recent initiatives for fiscal reform in 2010. The authors congratulate Washington state voters for resisting an economically damaging income tax ballot initiative and address how California's cap-and-trade plan promises to damage the state's economy, while doing little to affect greenhouse gas emissions. They also analyze more ubiquitous factors influencing state economies, such as escalating health care and labor costs.

In chapter 3, a simple roadmap for regaining state prosperity highlights the policies best suited for creating jobs and sparking economic growth. This chapter provides four key guiding principles lawmakers and other decision makers should follow to strengthen the economy in their states.

Finally, chapter 4 is the much anticipated 2011 ALEC-Laffer State Economic Competitiveness Index. The index provides two distinctive rankings for each state. The first, the Economic Performance Rank, is a backward looking measure based on a state's income per capita, absolute domestic migration, and nonfarm payroll employment—each of which is highly influenced by state policy. This ranking details states' individual performances over the past 10 years based on the economic data.

The second measure, the Economic Outlook Rank, is a forecast based on a state's current standing in 15 policy variables, each of which is influenced directly by state lawmakers through the legislative process. Generally, states that spend less, especially on income transfer programs, and states that tax less, particularly on productive activities, such as working or investing, experience higher growth rates than states that tax and spend more.

The following variables are measured in the 2011 ALEC-Laffer State Economic Outlook ranking:

Relationship Between Policies and Performance

ALEC-Laffer State Economic Outlook Rank vs. 10-Year Economic Performance, 1999-2009

State	Rank	Gross State Product Growth	Personal Income Growth	Personal Income Per Capita Growth	Population Growth
Utah	1	62.2%	59.8%	35.2%	24.1%
South Dakota	2	61.5%	56.1%	49.9%	7.5%
Virginia	3	55.1%	54.5%	46.2%	11.0%
Wyoming	4	119.8%	81.8%	70.7%	10.2%
Idaho	5	48.2%	53.5%	33.4%	18.9%
Colorado	6	45.9%	43.2%	30.8%	16.1%
North Dakota	7	73.3%	60.6%	69.5%	0.9%
Tennessee	8	36.2%	41.8%	32.7%	10.4%
Missouri	9	30.8%	38.6%	34.2%	6.8%
Florida	10	51.6%	54.8%	40.1%	15.5%
Top 10 Ranked States	-	**58.5%**	**54.5%**	**44.3%**	**12.1%**
Georgia	11	33.6%	42.9%	24.0%	19.4%
Arizona	12	56.9%	61.4%	32.6%	27.7%
Arkansas	13	47.8%	54.4%	48.9%	7.9%
Oklahoma	14	69.0%	55.5%	53.7%	6.7%
Louisiana	15	58.6%	60.5%	63.6%	0.5%
Indiana	16	30.0%	30.6%	28.7%	5.4%
Nevada	17	64.8%	59.2%	23.6%	31.0%
Texas	18	55.7%	60.3%	42.8%	18.3%
Mississippi	19	44.9%	46.2%	45.5%	3.6%
Alabama	20	45.1%	46.8%	43.5%	5.8%
Maryland	21	55.1%	49.3%	47.3%	7.3%
South Carolina	22	36.9%	46.9%	35.8%	13.4%
Iowa	23	46.2%	41.7%	44.4%	2.7%
Massachusetts	24	32.9%	34.7%	39.2%	3.6%
Michigan	25	7.2%	16.9%	21.2%	0.1%
North Carolina	26	41.7%	45.1%	30.4%	16.1%
Kansas	27	44.0%	44.0%	43.0%	4.7%
New Hampshire	28	33.7%	33.6%	34.2%	6.8%
Alaska	29	80.1%	57.5%	50.0%	11.3%
Wisconsin	30	34.6%	35.0%	33.2%	5.2%
West Virginia	31	50.3%	45.7%	50.6%	0.7%
Nebraska	32	47.8%	44.2%	41.5%	4.9%
Washington	33	47.6%	49.1%	36.2%	12.7%
Delaware	34	44.9%	43.7%	35.1%	12.6%
Connecticut	35	34.4%	36.0%	39.6%	3.1%
Montana	36	64.6%	60.2%	55.7%	7.9%
Minnesota	37	36.7%	37.0%	34.6%	6.7%
Ohio	38	22.3%	25.3%	28.1%	1.6%
New Mexico	39	48.0%	61.4%	53.6%	10.4%
Kentucky	40	36.6%	38.7%	38.6%	6.6%
Pennsylvania	41	38.4%	36.9%	40.5%	2.6%
Rhode Island	42	42.0%	40.7%	47.1%	0.2%
Oregon	43	46.2%	40.5%	30.9%	11.5%
Illinois	44	30.9%	33.1%	34.8%	3.8%
New Jersey	45	36.9%	33.5%	39.4%	3.3%
Hawaii	46	58.8%	55.0%	50.7%	6.9%
California	47	43.0%	38.0%	34.7%	8.7%
Maine	48	39.2%	41.3%	44.4%	3.2%
Vermont	49	39.3%	41.8%	46.8%	1.9%
New York	50	40.8%	38.2%	42.6%	2.9%
Lowest 10 Ranked States	-	**41.6%**	**39.9%**	**41.2%**	**4.5%**
U.S. Average	-	**47.0%**	**46.2%**	**41.1%**	**8.6%**

Net Domestic in-Migration as % of Population	Non-Farm Payroll Employment Growth	2010 Unemployment Rate
2.0%	11.8%	7.7%
0.8%	7.3%	4.8%
2.2%	4.4%	6.9%
4.1%	19.4%	7.0%
7.4%	10.7%	9.3%
4.1%	2.6%	8.9%
-2.9%	12.5%	3.9%
4.3%	-4.3%	9.7%
0.7%	-2.9%	9.6%
6.9%	3.9%	11.5%
3.0%	**6.5%**	**7.9%**
5.8%	-2.0%	10.2%
11.1%	8.9%	9.9%
2.6%	0.4%	7.9%
1.0%	3.3%	7.1%
-6.8%	-1.1%	7.5%
-0.4%	-7.7%	10.2%
14.2%	12.4%	14.9%
3.5%	10.5%	8.2%
-1.2%	-5.9%	10.4%
1.8%	-3.1%	9.5%
-1.7%	3.2%	7.5%
6.8%	-2.2%	11.2%
-1.7%	-0.5%	6.1%
-4.9%	-3.9%	8.5%
-5.6%	-16.5%	12.5%
6.9%	0.3%	10.5%
-2.4%	-0.6%	7.0%
2.3%	1.7%	6.1%
-1.1%	15.0%	8.0%
-0.3%	-3.4%	8.3%
0.9%	0.8%	9.1%
-2.2%	3.6%	4.6%
3.5%	4.0%	9.6%
5.2%	-1.7%	8.5%
-2.8%	-3.8%	9.1%
4.0%	10.2%	7.2%
-1.0%	-0.9%	7.3%
-3.4%	-10.7%	10.1%
1.5%	9.8%	8.4%
1.9%	-2.5%	10.4%
-0.4%	-1.0%	8.7%
-4.3%	-3.8%	11.6%
4.6%	-0.6%	10.8%
-5.1%	-7.0%	10.3%
-5.3%	-1.8%	9.4%
-2.2%	8.6%	6.6%
-4.0%	-2.3%	12.4%
2.0%	-0.7%	7.9%
-0.5%	0.2%	6.2%
-8.6%	-0.5%	8.5%
-2.4%	**-0.9%**	**9.2%**
0.9%	1.5%	8.8%

- Highest Marginal Personal Income Tax Rate
- Highest Marginal Corporate Income Tax Rate
- Personal Income Tax Progressivity
- Property Tax Burden
- Sales Tax Burden
- Tax Burden from All Remaining Taxes
- Estate Tax/Inheritance Tax (Yes or No)
- Recently Legislated Tax Policy Changes
- Debt Service as a Share of Tax Revenue
- Public Employees per 1,000 Residents
- Quality of State Legal System
- State Minimum Wage
- Workers' Compensation Costs
- Right-to-Work State (Yes or No)
- Tax or Expenditure Limits

This fourth edition of *Rich States, Poor States* provides 50 unique snapshots of state economies for your evaluation. Study the rankings and read the evidence and you will discover the principles for state economic prosperity.

Enjoy.

10 Golden Rules
of Effective Taxation

1 *When you tax something more you get less of it, and when you tax something less you get more of it.*

Tax policy is all about reward and punishment. Most politicians know instinctively that taxes reduce the activity being taxed—even if they do not care to admit it. Congress and state lawmakers routinely tax things that they consider "bad" to discourage the activity. We reduce, or in some cases entirely eliminate, taxes on behavior that we want to encourage, such as home buying, going to college, giving money to charity, and so on. By lowering the tax rate in some cases to zero, we lower the after tax cost, in the hopes that this will lead more people to engage in a desirable activity.

It is wise to keep taxes on work, savings, and investment as low as possible in order not to deter people from participating in these activities.

2 *Individuals work and produce goods and services to earn money for present or future consumption.*

Workers save, but they do so for the purpose of conserving resources so they or their children can consume in the future. A corollary to this is that people do not work to pay taxes—though some politicians seem to think they do.

3 *Taxes create a wedge between the cost of working and the rewards from working.*

To state this in economic terms, the difference between the price paid by people who demand goods and services for consumption and the price received by people who provide these goods and services—the suppliers—is called the wedge. Income and other payroll taxes, as well as regulations, restrictions, and government requirements, separate the wages employers pay from the wages employees receive. If a worker pays 15 percent of his income in payroll taxes, 25 percent in federal income taxes, and 5 percent in state income taxes, his $50,000 wage is reduced to roughly $27,500 after taxes. The lost $22,500 of income is the tax wedge, or approximately 45 percent. As large as the wedge seems in this example, it is just part of the total wedge. The wedge also includes excise, sales, and property taxes, plus an assortment of costs, such as the market value of the accountants and lawyers hired to maintain compliance with government regulations. As the wedge grows, the total cost to a firm of employing a person goes up, but the net payment received by the person goes down. Thus, both the quantity of labor demanded and quantity supplied fall to a new, lower equilibrium level, and a lower level of economic activity ensues. This is why all taxes ultimately affect people's incentive to work and invest, though some taxes clearly have a more detrimental effect than others.

4 *An increase in tax rates will not lead to a dollar-for-dollar increase in tax revenues, and a reduction in tax rates that encourages production will lead to less than a dollar-for-dollar reduction in tax revenues.*

Lower marginal tax rates reduce the tax wedge and lead to an expansion in the production base and improved resource allocation. Thus, while less tax revenue may be collected per unit of tax base, the tax base itself increases. This expansion of the tax base will, therefore, offset some (and in some cases, all) of the loss in revenues because of the now lower rates.

Tax rate changes also affect the amount of tax avoidance. It is important to note that legal tax avoidance is differentiated throughout this report from illegal tax evasion. The higher the marginal tax rate, the greater the incentive to reduce taxable income. Tax avoidance takes many forms, from workers electing to take an improvement in nontaxable fringe benefits in lieu of higher gross wages to investment in tax shelter programs. Business decisions, too, are increasingly based on tax considerations as opposed to market efficiency. For example, the incentive to avoid a 40 percent tax, which takes $40 of every $100 earned, is twice as high as the incentive to avoid a 20 percent tax, for which a worker forfeits $20 of every $100 earned.

An obvious way to avoid paying a tax is to eliminate market transactions upon which the tax is applied. This can be accomplished through vertical integration: Manufacturers can establish wholesale outlets; retailers can purchase goods directly from manufacturers; companies can acquire suppliers or distributors. The number of steps remains the same, but fewer and fewer steps involve market transactions and thereby avoid the tax. If states refrain from applying their sales taxes on business-to-business transactions, they will avoid the numerous economic distortions caused by tax cascading. Michigan, for example, should not tax the sale of rubber to a tire company, then tax the tire when it is sold to the auto company, then tax the sale of the car from the auto company to the dealer, then tax the dealer's sale of the car to the final purchaser of the car, or the rubber and wheels are taxed multiple times. Additionally, the tax cost becomes embedded in the price of the product and remains hidden from the consumer.

5 *If tax rates become too high, they may lead to a reduction in tax receipts. The relationship between tax rates and tax receipts has been described by the Laffer Curve.*

The Laffer Curve (illustrated below) summarizes this phenomenon. We start this curve with the undeniable fact that there are two tax rates that generate zero tax revenues: a zero tax rate and a 100 percent tax rate. (Remember Golden Rule #2: People don't work for the privilege of paying taxes, so if all their earnings are taken in taxes, they do not work, or at least they do not earn income the government knows about. And, thus, the government receives no revenues.)

Now, within what is referred to as the "normal range," an increase in tax rates will lead to an increase in tax revenues. At some point, however, higher tax rates become counterproductive. Above this point, called the "prohibitive range," an increase in tax rates leads to a reduction in tax revenues and vice versa. Over the entire range, with a tax rate reduction, the revenues collected per dollar of tax base falls. This is the arithmetic effect. But the number of units in the tax base expands. Lower tax rates lead to higher levels of personal income, employment, retail sales, investment, and general economic activity. This is the economic, or incentive, effect. Tax avoidance also declines. In the normal range, the arithmetic effect of a tax rate reduction dominates. In the prohibitive range, the economic effect is dominant.

The Laffer Curve

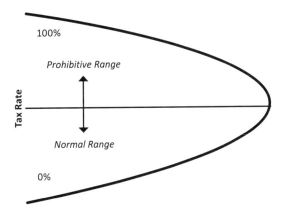

Source: Laffer Associates

Of course, where a state's tax rate lies along the Laffer Curve depends on many factors, including tax rates in neighboring jurisdictions. If a state with a high employment or payroll tax borders a state with large population centers along that border, businesses will have an incentive to shift their operations from inside the jurisdiction of the high tax state to the jurisdiction of the low-tax state.

Economists have observed a clear Laffer Curve effect with respect to cigarette taxes. States with high tobacco taxes that are located next to states with low tobacco taxes have very low retail sales of cigarettes relative to the low tax states. Illinois smokers buy many cartons of cigarettes when in Indiana, and the retail sales of cigarettes in the two states show this.

6 *The more mobile the factors being taxed, the larger the response to a change in tax rates. The less mobile the factor, the smaller the change in the tax base for a given change in tax rates.*

Taxes on capital are almost impossible to enforce in the 21st century because capital is instantly transportable. For example, imagine the behavior of an entrepreneur or corporation that builds a factory at a time when profit taxes are low. Once the factory is built, the low rate is raised substantially without warning. The owners of the factory may feel cheated by the tax bait and switch, but they probably do not shut the factory down because it still earns a positive after tax profit. The factory will remain in operation for a time even though the rate of return, after tax, has fallen sharply. If the factory were to be shut down, the after tax return would be zero. After some time has passed, when equipment needs servicing, the lower rate of return will discourage further investment, and the plant will eventually move where tax rates are lower.

A study by the American Enterprise Institute has found that high corporate income taxes at the national level are associated with lower growth in wages. Again, it appears a chain reaction occurs when corporate taxes get too high. Capital moves out of the high tax area, but wages are a function of the ratio of capital to labor, so the reduction in capital decreases the wage rate.

The distinction between initial impact and burden was perhaps best explained by one of our favorite 20th century economists, Nobel winner Friedrich A. Hayek, who makes the point as follows in his classic, *The Constitution of Liberty*:

> *The illusion that by some means of progressive taxation the burden can be shifted substantially onto the shoulders of the wealthy has been the chief reason why taxation has increased as fast as it has done and that, under the influence of this illusion, the masses have come to accept a much heavier load than they would have done otherwise. The only major result of the policy has been the severe limitation of the incomes that could be earned by the most successful and thereby gratification of the envy of the less well off.*

7 *Raising tax rates on one source of revenue may reduce the tax revenue from other sources, while reducing the tax rate on one activity may raise the taxes raised from other activities.*

For example, an increase in the tax rate on corporate profits would be expected to lead to a diminution in the amount of corporate activity, and hence profits, within the taxing district. That alone implies less than a proportionate increase in corporate tax revenues. Such a reduction in corporate activity also implies a reduction in employment and personal income. As a result, personal income tax revenues would fall. This decline, too, could offset the increase in corporate tax revenues. Conversely, a reduction in corporate tax rates may lead to a less than expected loss in revenues and an increase in tax receipts from other sources.

8 *An economically efficient tax system has a sensible, broad tax base and a low tax rate.*

Ideally, the tax system of a state, city, or country will distort economic activity only minimally. High tax rates alter economic behavior. Ronald Reagan used to tell the story that he would stop making movies during his acting career once he was in the 90 percent tax bracket because the income he received was so low after taxes were taken away. If the tax base is broad, tax rates can be kept as low and nonconfiscatory as possible. This is one reason we favor a flat tax with minimal deductions and loopholes. It is also why 24 nations have now adopted a flat tax.

9 *Income transfer (welfare) payments also create a de facto tax on work and, thus, have a high impact on the vitality of a state's economy.*

Unemployment benefits, welfare payments, and subsidies all represent a redistribution of income. For every transfer recipient, there is an equivalent tax payment or future tax liability. Thus, income effects cancel. In many instances, these payments are given to people only in the absence of work or output. Examples include food stamps (income tests), Social Security benefits (retirement test), agricultural subsidies, and, of course, unemployment compensation itself. Thus, the wedge on work effort is growing at the same time that subsidies for not working are increasing. Transfer payments represent a tax on production and a subsidy to leisure. Their automatic increase in the event of a fall in market income leads to an even sharper drop in output.

In some high benefit states, such as Hawaii, Massachusetts, and New York, the entire package of welfare payments can pay people the equivalent of a $10 per hour job (and let us not forget: welfare benefits are not taxed, but wages and salaries are). Because these benefits shrink as income levels from work climb, welfare can impose very high marginal tax rates (60 percent or more) on low-income Americans. And those disincentives to work have a deleterious effect. We found a high, statistically significant, negative relationship between the level of benefits in a state and the percentage reduction in caseloads.

In sum, high welfare benefits magnify the tax wedge between effort and reward. As such, output is expected to fall as a consequence of making benefits from not working more generous. Thus, an increase in unemployment benefits is expected to lead to a rise in unemployment.

Finally, and most important of all for state legislators to remember:

10 *If A and B are two locations, and if taxes are raised in B and lowered in A, producers and manufacturers will have a greater incentive to move from B to A.*

Denver, Colorado

The State of the States

The State of the States

Big, maybe even seismic, changes are coming to the states and the way they operate from 2011 forward. The tremors from the Republican landslide elections in November 2010 were felt most deeply at the state level, with a Republican net pickup of roughly 700 seats in the state legislatures around the country. There are now nearly 30 newly elected governors—from New Mexico to Ohio to Maine—most of whom entered office with a new governing philosophy oriented toward free markets, limited government, lower tax rates, and business-friendly policies.

Rick Scott, the new governor of Florida, represents this new governing philosophy as well as anyone. He is new to public office and disparaging of life-long politicians. He says, "we are going to make Florida a pro-business and pro-competitive state, so when a firm looks to operate in North America, they think of Florida first." He says he admires Rick Perry's success in Texas and Chris Christie's achievements in New Jersey. "We are going to learn what Texas and New Jersey have done, and in Florida, we are going to do it better."[1]

He is going to have to compete against other newcomers with an agenda for change. That long list of reformers includes Scott Walker of Wisconsin, John Kasich of Ohio, Robert Bentley of Alabama, Mary Fallin of Oklahoma, and Sam Brownback of Kansas. Even New York Democrat Andrew Cuomo is talking about protecting taxpayers, taking on the public sector unions, streamlining government services, and fixing schools.

The State of State Finances

The other big story of 2011 will be how states deal with continued budget deficits, which are largely a result of two decades of fiscal profligacy.[2]

Of course, some on the Left would like to blame strictly a shortage of tax revenue for the budget gaps in the states. However, there are two sides of the fiscal coin, and it is clear a vast majority of states set themselves up to fail by spending beyond their means and hoping the market will keep up with their spending sprees. According to the Mercatus Center at George Mason University, "Rapid growth in per capita spending, a lack of economic freedom, and weak balanced budget rules caused the (budget) gaps. The recession just exposed these underlying problems."[3] The study, which analyzes two decades of state budget data, suggests—all other factors being equal—that states spending the most over the period had budget gaps nearly 20 percent greater than the most austere states.[4] From 1985 to 2005, most state budgets doubled, and some tripled, in size.[5] In the past decade alone, state and local budgets grew 90 percent faster than the private sector's Gross Domestic Product (GDP).[6]

Again, the academic statistics back up what we all know is the key to good budgeting: the ability to say no. Furthermore, the American people understand this growth in spending simply is not sustainable. When asked what to blame for current budget problems, an overwhelming 75 percent of Americans say politicians' unwillingness to cut spending.[7]

States will have to fend for themselves financially this year: Almost all of the fiscal stimulus money from 2008–2009 has already been spent, and the new Republican majority in the U.S. House of Representatives is unlikely to appropriate more bailout dollars for state budgets. States that took federal stimulus money also agreed to "maintenance of effort" provisions, which prohibit them from downsizing many programs going forward, compounding the problem. This is why the 2010 edition of this publication warned states that federal "free" stimulus money would be a curse, not a blessing.[8] That prognosis has turned out to be correct—to the detriment of state lawmakers working toward real budget reform. In the end, Milton Friedman had it right: With government, there is no such thing as a free lunch.

The good news is that states may finally get a respite from the dismal fiscal picture of the last two years. State tax revenues began to pick up in late 2010 and are looking strong in early 2011, thanks in part to the extension of the Bush tax cuts at the federal level, which should help spur economic growth, and lessen the risk of a double-dip recession.[9] Researchers at the Rockefeller Institute of Government report that revenue was up 4.5 percent in the third quarter of 2010.[10] Even more encouraging is that preliminary numbers show stronger revenue growth from the first part of 2011. According to the Rockefeller Institute, "several important indicators suggest broad state fiscal conditions remain fragile. These include the record revenue declines during the Great Recession, continued upward trends in state spending, and unemployment rates that remain nearly double their pre-recession levels, to name a few."[11] Indeed, it will take many more quarters of positive revenue growth to return to fiscal stability. According to a 2010 Government Accountability Office (GAO) study, the state and local government sector will face a $9.9 trillion budget gap over the next few decades.[12]

One solution many governors, including Chris Christie of New Jersey, Rick Perry of Texas, and Bob McDonnell of Virginia, have implemented is to reset budget baselines to 2007 levels to reflect the "new normal" of mediocre revenue collections.[13] We think nearly every state will need a budget reset back to 2007 or 2008 levels to avoid permanent deficits.

Wisconsin Exposes Deeper State Budget Crisis

In the wake of the recent protests in Wisconsin and several other states, Americans are taking a much closer look at the grim budget realities facing our states today. Wisconsin governor Scott Walker correctly points out that his state's current budget trajectory is unsustainable, and he is not alone.

The financial state of the states is not encouraging. Driven by irresponsible state and local spending growth, which have steadily outpaced private sector growth over the past decade, current budget deficits are estimated to exceed $100 billion in the upcoming fiscal year.

As bad as they are, these budget gaps are overshadowed in size and scope by unfunded liabilities in state pension and health care systems for public employees, which are *trillions* of dollars in the red.[14] These are unsustainable cost drivers that threaten the financial solvency of the states. Without fundamental pension reform, expect the news stories discussing the possibility of state bankruptcy to continue.[15]

As liberal former California Speaker Willie Brown recently put it, "At some point, someone is going to have to get honest about the fact that 80 percent of the state, county, and city budget deficits are due to employee costs. Either we do something about it at the ballot box, or a judge will do something about it in bankruptcy court."[16]

The problem is that most of the legislative "fixes" over the past few years for state budgets

---

⊢ Steps to a Priority-Based Budget ⊢

To gain control of a state budget, the following questions should be answered:

What is the role of government?
What are the essential services the government must provide to fulfill its purpose?
How will we know if government is doing a good job?
What should all of this cost?
When cuts must be made, how will they be properly prioritized?

have merely kicked the can down the road, postponing or obscuring problems rather than solving them.[17] That has to end, and, as Speaker Brown suggests, everything has to be on the table, including a review of public employee pay and benefits.

ALEC just released its State Budget Reform Toolkit to help in this effort, providing state legislators with more than 20 recommendations for modernizing state budgets, improving budget transparency, controlling costs, and improving government efficiency.[18] By setting clear priorities and getting their public employee costs under control, states can show they are able to live within their means, just like taxpayers do.

States need innovative budgeting strategies to address these new economic challenges without resorting to economically damaging tax increases; they must move toward building priority-based budgets. In 2003, a bipartisan group of legislators in Washington state, along with Democrat Gov. Gary Locke, successfully implemented priority-based budgeting to eliminate a budget deficit of more than $2 billion.[19]

Only by carefully considering the proper role of government can legislators and governors effectively protect individual rights while providing essential services to taxpayers in an efficient, cost-effective manner. Great savings can be achieved if legislators and agencies focus on the core functions of government instead of wasting time determining how a nonessential function can be better performed. Despite the economic difficulties facing the states, there is a pathway to budget reform and financial sustainability.

America's Protected Class

According to the Bureau of Labor Statistics at the U.S. Department of Labor, as of December 2010, state and local government employees not only earned more in wages than their private sector counterparts, but they also received benefits 69 percent higher than those in the private sector.[20] If states could grow money on trees, it would be grand for politicians to hand out Cadillac benefit plans to all workers, but in a world of limited resources, states must choose between needs and wants.

Years ago, the private sector transitioned away from the defined-benefit model of pensions for its workers because it could not sustain the costs

and be profitable. Today, it is estimated that only 21 percent of private sector employers offer a defined-benefit pension.[21] In contrast, in the protected class of state and local government employment, approximately 84 percent of employees still receive a defined-benefit pension, and in some cases, the employees do not contribute a dollar themselves.[22] This unsustainable defined-benefit model has resulted in a financial catastrophe for state taxpayers. As *The Wall Street Journal*'s Daniel Henninger put it, "Americans, staring at fiscal crevasses opening across Europe, have to decide if they also wish to spend the next 50 years laboring mainly to produce tax revenue to pay for public workers' pensions and other public promises. The private sector would exist for the public sector."[23] As Maryland delegate Melony Griffith (who, according to Project Vote Smart, was previously rated 100 percent supportive by the Maryland teachers' union) said, "It's no surprise that people would like to have a more beneficial package, but quite honestly we can't afford it."[24]

FIGURE 1

State and Local Government Employees Costs per Hour Worked (December 2010)

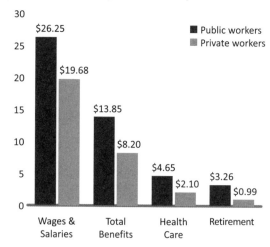

Source: U.S. Bureau of Labor Statistics

Our friends at State Budget Solutions have put together a valuable chart outlining the various estimates of unfunded pension liabilities by state. As shown in Table 1 on the following page, the estimates range from a low $450 billion from the PEW Center for the States to nearly $3 trillion

Table 1 | **State Unfunded Pension Liabilities**

Source: State Budget Solutions

State	PEW Study	AEI Study	Novy-Marx and Rauh Study
Alabama	$9,228,918,000	$43,544,880,000	$40,400,000,000
Alaska	$3,522,661,000	$14,192,229,000	$9,300,000,000
Arizona	$7,871,120,000	$45,004,090,000	$48,700,000,000
Arkansas	$2,752,546,000	$20,026,314,000	$15,800,000,000
California	$59,492,498,000	$398,490,573,000	$370,100,000,000
Colorado	$16,813,048,000	$71,387,842,000	$57,400,000,000
Connecticut	$15,858,500,000	$48,515,241,000	$4,900,000,000
Delaware	$129,359,000	$5,688,663,000	$5,100,000,000
Florida	($1,798,789,000)*	$98,505,110,000	$8,980,000,000
Georgia	$6,384,903,000	$58,742,784,000	$57,000,000,000
Hawaii	$5,168,108,000	$18,533,398,000	$16,100,000,000
Idaho	$772,200,000	$10,022,613,000	$7,900,000,000
Illinois	$54,383,939,000	$192,458,660,000	$167,300,000,000
Indiana	$9,825,830,000	$33,756,655,000	$30,200,000,000
Iowa	$2,694,794,000	$21,266,226,000	$17,000,000,000
Kansas	$8,279,168,000	$21,827,991,000	$20,100,000,000
Kentucky	$12,328,429,000	$47,016,382,000	$42,300,000,000
Louisiana	$11,658,734,000	$43,797,899,000	$36,400,000,000
Maine	$2,782,173,000	$13,227,289,000	$11,800,000,000
Maryland	$10,926,099,000	$48,199,258,000	$43,500,000,000
Massachusetts	$21,759,452,000	$60,476,274,000	$54,200,000,000
Michigan	$11,514,600,000	$72,187,197,000	$63,600,000,000
Minnesota	$10,771,507,000	$59,354,330,000	$55,100,000,000
Mississippi	$7,971,277,000	$32,225,716,000	$28,700,000,000
Missouri	$9,025,293,000	$56,760,147,000	$42,100,000,000
Montana	$1,549,503,000	$8,633,301,000	$7,100,000,000
Nebraska	$754,748,000	$7,438,589,000	$6,100,000,000
Nevada	$7,281,752,000	$33,529,346,000	$17,500,000,000
New Hampshire	$2,522,175,000	$10,233,796,000	$8,200,000,000
New Jersey	$34,434,055,000	$144,869,687,000	$124,000,000,000
New Mexico	$4,519,887,000	$27,875,180,000	$23,900,000,000
New York	($10,428,000,000)	$182,350,104,000	$132,900,000,000
North Carolina	$504,760,000	$48,898,412,000	$37,800,000,000
North Dakota	$546,500,000	$4,099,053,000	$3,600,000,000
Ohio	$19,502,065,000	$187,793,480,000	$166,700,000,000
Oklahoma	$13,172,407,000	$33,647,372,000	$30,100,000,000
Oregon	$10,739,000,000	$42,203,565,000	$37,800,000,000
Pennsylvania	$13,724,480,000	$114,144,897,000	$100,200,000,000
Rhode Island	$4,353,892,000	$15,005,840,000	$13,900,000,000
South Carolina	$12,052,684,000	$36,268,910,000	$43,200,000,000
South Dakota	$182,870,000	$5,982,103,000	$4,700,000,000
Tennessee	$1,602,802,000	$30,546,099,000	$23,200,000,000
Texas	$13,781,228,000	$180,720,642,000	$142,300,000,000
Utah	$3,611,399,000	$18,626,024,000	$16,500,000,000
Vermont	$461,551,000	$3,602,752,000	$3,300,000,000
Virginia	$10,723,000,000	$53,783,973,000	$48,300,000,000
Washington	($179,100,000)	$51,807,902,000	$42,900,000,000
West Virginia	$4,968,709,000	$14,378,914,000	$11,100,000,000
Wisconsin	$252,600,000	$62,691,675,000	$56,200,000,000
Wyoming	$1,444,353,000	$6,628,204,000	$5,400,000,000
Total U.S.	**$452,195,687,000**	**$2,860,967,583,000**	**$2,485,800,000,000**

*Parenthesis indicates surplus in state pension funds. Please reference endnote 25.

from the American Enterprise Institute.[25] We believe the accurate estimate is much closer to the $3 trillion figure.

Critics of real pension reform might suggest that pension systems can grow their way out of their unfunded liabilities. For that to be the case requires making the most optimistic assumptions and assumes future politicians will not continue the age-old process of raiding pension funds for general fund use. If executives in the private sector tried that approach, federal authorities would have a home waiting for them in a place like Leavenworth, Kan.

Many official estimates of the size and scope of state and local government employee pension liabilities are miles from reality. Here are a few major reasons we are bearish on the ability of states to escape the pension crisis without fundamental reform.

Warren Buffett recently said states are being far too rosy in their expectations of the future market performance for their assets. Unbelievably, some states still assume an average rate of return of 8-9 percent.[26] Don't we all wish we could simply assume such rates of return? Mr. Buffett, the "Oracle of Omaha," says states should use a much more conservative assumed future growth rate to accurately value their pension liabilities in this era of new market realities.[27] Bill Gates Jr., who spent the last year studying the issue, has observed that states must rethink their pension systems and do away with their pension "gimmicks." [28]

The other major reason state and local pension funds are in precarious financial shape is due to the devastating market losses pension funds suffered during the 2008 financial crisis. Many funds, driven into riskier and riskier investment choices by attempting to meet the unrealistic rates of return mentioned above, lost 25 to nearly 30 percent of their entire assets in 2008. The city of Detroit gambled on risky investment choices like an airline company that has undergone three bankruptcies and a luxury Detroit hotel. According to a recent news report, the Securities and Exchange Commission is currently investigating the city.[29]

In many cases, these losses have not yet fully been accounted for in official unfunded liability estimates. You may be surprised to know that states can use "flexible" guidelines of the Governmental Accounting Standards Board (GASB), which allow them to "smooth" the 2008 pension fund losses for 5–8 years in some cases. This means we are only starting to begin to realize the dramatic losses from 2008. Those who say states will easily be able to make up these losses better hope for market returns able to beat Warren Buffett's projections over the next 30 years.

For the reasons outlined, we think the more bearish estimates of unfunded pension fund liabilities in Table 1 are probably closest to the truth. As the old saying goes "whenever government says a problem is bad, the reality is almost always worse." Some on the Left may continue to deny that pension funds face a funding crisis, but states should beware; they ignore this debt tsunami at their own peril.

Pension Reform Gains Momentum

In response to mounting unfunded liabilities, many states are increasingly considering replacing their defined-benefit pension plans with 401(k)-style defined-contribution plans for new employees.[30] ALEC member Senator Dan Liljenquist of Utah spearheaded a major pension reform that is undoubtedly one of the most important legislative accomplishments on fiscal reform anywhere in America in recent years. According to Sen. Liljenquist's congressional testimony:

> Utah closed its defined-benefit pension plans to new enrollees, creating a new retirement system for new employees hired after July 1, 2011. Under Utah's new retirement system, public employees will receive a defined employer contribution towards retirement. New public employees will be able to choose between (1) a 401(k) style program, or (2) a hybrid pension program (where they may pool market risk with other employees). Regardless of the program employees choose, Utah will only contribute at a set amount towards retirement. Utah's recent pension reforms will, over time, reduce and eliminate Utah's pension related bankruptcy risk. This is a big win for Utah taxpayers.[31]

We could not agree more, and we hope many other states will follow Utah's lead and protect taxpayers from being forced to pick up the tab for the massive unfunded liabilities in many grossly neglected public pension funds.

State Competitiveness

America's new governors and state lawmakers seem to understand what we have been saying in this report for years: State policies matter in terms of which states prosper and which states fall behind in the race for jobs and economic growth. The policy blunders that hurt growth prospects the most are high income tax rates, forced union work rules, heavy regulation, an excessive state workforce, unfunded public pensions and health plans, poorly performing schools, and a litigation system that invites expensive and frivolous lawsuits. Two new policy mistakes, now in vogue in many state capitals that will cost their states jobs and make their citizens poorer, should be added to this list. The first is state based cap-and-trade taxes to address climate change. Regardless of what one thinks about global warming, it does not make sense for a state to unilaterally disarm its economic competitiveness through such a tax regime. State cap-and-trade laws—California has the most onerous—do not reduce global carbon emissions. They simply move factories out of a state, or out of the country, to places that do not have cap-and-trade laws.

The second reckless policy is setting a state renewable energy standard. The evidence is clear that policies requiring a state to get 20 percent, or even 33 percent, of its electricity from so-called "green energy" only increase electricity prices substantially for families and businesses in the state. California's renewable energy requirement is forecast to cost state electric users roughly $12 billion in the short term—money taxpayers in this economically debilitated state cannot possibly afford right now.[32] The wrongheadedness of renewable energy laws is compounded by the fact that reliance on wind power, as Colorado has discovered, fails to reduce carbon emissions much, if at all. Wind is such an unreliable source of electricity that coal plants are required to operate around the clock as a backup for wind power.[33]

The False Promise of Green Jobs

A new study finds that 140 major businesses moved out of the Golden State in 2010, three times the pace of outmigration in 2009.[34] Things will not get any better for a while in California, thanks to a new voter approved law to impose a cap-and-trade climate change regime on the state's utilities and industries. This state is already untold billions of dollars in debt. We retell the story so others can avoid this dose of economic cyanide.

From the 1950s through the 1990s, California was a golden land of economic opportunity, but no more. In 2007, Gov. Arnold Schwarzenegger signed the law AB 32, which he said would propel California into an economy expanding, green job future. Well, a new study by the state's own auditing agency burst that green bubble.

The study, released May 13, 2010, concludes that "California's economy at large will likely be adversely affected in the near term by implementing climate related policies that are not adopted elsewhere." While the long term economic costs are "unknown," the study finds that AB 32 will raise energy prices, "causing the prices of goods and services to rise; lowering business profits; and reducing production, income and jobs."[35] That is pretty straightforward.

The economic reality here is what the Legislative Analyst's Office calls "economic leakage." That is jargon for businesses and jobs that will "locate or relocate outside the state of California where regulatory related costs are lower." The study says the negative impact on most California industries will be "modest," but energy intensive industries—specifically, aluminum, chemicals, forest products, oil, gas, and steel—"may significantly reduce their business activity in California."[36] The prediction was fairly accurate. Yes, some new "green jobs" will be created, but the "net economy wide impact," it says, "will in all likelihood be negative."[37]

Enough Californian voters either ignored the report or shrugged and decided such costs are worth it to save the planet from CO_2. But the report bursts that bubble too, concluding that the California law's impact on carbon emissions will be *de minimis* because "the economic activity that is shifted will also generate" greenhouse gasses outside the state. Recognizing this problem, California politicians are busy trying to get a Western regional pact to reduce carbon emissions, but so far Arizona, Montana, Oregon, Utah, and Washington have refused. They would rather have the jobs.

We hope they do not get suckered into this policy. It should be obvious to state legislators that similar job and business "leakage" will strike the United States in general if cap-and-trade passes in their state. The hardest hit industries will leave cap-and-trade states and relocate to the likes of China and India where marginal costs are lower. States that want to stop outsourcing need to avoid taxing their own industries.

Sadly, California has joined the ranks of the "has been" states, and its outmigration problem has only gotten worse in the past years. Despite all of its natural geographical advantages—ports of entry to the Pacific region, balmy weather, relaxing beaches, idyllic mountains, and as the Beach Boys sang, those gorgeous "California Girls"—years of redistributionist economic policies have resulted in more U.S. residents leaving California than arriving there. As we will go into more detail later in this chapter, the decline of California is probably the best evidence we can present to show the impact of poor policy decisions on a state's economic pulse.

Cheerful News from the States

Fortunately, not all news is bad in the states this year. Despite persistent budget shortfalls caused by overspending, many states are taking steps to become more competitive for business and job growth. We continue to anticipate which state will be the first to eliminate its income tax since Alaska eliminated its income tax several decades ago. There are states that have the political alignment to get this done, and we would not be surprised if one of the southern states—perhaps South Carolina, Georgia, or Alabama—phased out their state income tax. Also, as outlined in last year's "Missouri Compromise" chapter of this publication, the Show-Me State is seriously considering joining the ranks of the no income tax states, largely in the quest to become a growth state for jobs.[38] Whichever state eliminates its income tax first will send a blaring message to the rest of the country: Our state is open for business.

Among pro-growth tax reform proposals so far in 2011:

- Though Missouri has not yet repealed its income tax, Show-Me State lawmakers just repealed the state's anti-business franchise tax, and Gov. Jay Nixon, a Democrat, signed this legislation (SB 19) into law. "Once fully phased out, SB 19 will save Missouri employers more than $80 million annually, money that employers can instead invest in expanding businesses and creating jobs and

opportunity for working Missourians," said Daniel P. Mehan, Missouri Chamber president and CEO.[39]

- Rep. Ed Garner introduced a bill that effectively would have eliminated the capital gains tax on new investment in Arkansas. After passing the Democrat controlled Arkansas House of Representatives, the bill unfortunately died on a voice vote in a Senate committee.[40] The Arkansas Department of Finance and Administration, the state's revenue scoring agency, almost laughably scored the legislation as a huge revenue loss and then officially testified in opposition to this pro-growth legislation that would have made Arkansas more competitive. What a shame, not to mention a lost opportunity to make Arkansas a more prosperous state. This sort of taxpayer funded lobbying needs to be discontinued in short order.

- You can add Oklahoma to the list of states considering eliminating its income tax. "We're going to have to do something drastic to move the state forward," State Rep. David Dank said. "We would be able to recruit more industry, get more productive people in here making money, spending money and it would really be a benefit to our economy."[41] The Oklahoma Senate took that pro-growth idea a step further and actually passed the legislation to eliminate the state's income tax.[42]

- Hoping to keep pace with their neighbors to the south, legislators in Kansas recently passed important pro-growth legislation that would automatically phase down personal and corporate income tax rates. Under the proposal—the March to Economic Growth Act—which passed the House but stalled in the Senate, taxpayers would enjoy reduced income tax rates on personal and corporate taxes when state revenue grows. "It would begin the process of Kansas becoming a pro-growth state," Rep. Richard Carlson, Chairman of the House Taxation Committee, said.[43]

- North Dakota lawmakers are sparring with Gov. Jack Dalrymple and rejected his tax relief proposal—because it was not large enough! As it turns out, the Legislature's plan would slash personal income tax rates by 20 percent and reduce corporate tax rates by 10 percent.[44]

- The Iowa House passed a 20 percent across the board tax reduction on the personal income tax.[45] As Majority Leader Linda Upmeyer said, "This bill will allow employers to put Iowans back to work, inject millions of dollars into Iowa's economy and get our state moving forward again."[46]

- The Arizona Legislature recently approved a significant cut to their corporate tax rate as well. After signing the bill, which will reduce the state's corporate rate from nearly 7 percent to 4.9 percent, Gov. Jan Brewer said, "I'm not willing to stand aside and just wait until the Arizona economy recovers."[47]

- Michigan Governor Rick Snyder has proposed, and the Legislature has approved, a plan to enhance his state's competitiveness by eliminating the onerous Michigan Business Tax. This tax has been a noose around the neck of Michigan's economic recovery since it replaced another barrier to growth—Michigan's burdensome Single Business Tax—less than five years ago.[48] The Wolverine State should be first in line for policies to increase competitiveness after losing a decade's worth of growth under Jennifer Granholm's tax happy administration.

- Lawmakers in the Hoosier State voted to reduce their corporate income tax from 8.5 percent to 6.5 percent. State Rep. Eric Turner described the necessity of making Indiana more competitive through this tax relief. "It creates sticker shock when companies are looking at Indiana," he said. "This is the jobs bill—not corporate welfare."[49]

- In Florida, Gov. Rick Scott crafted "Florida's first jobs budget," which reduces state spending by $4.6 billion and cuts taxes by $3.6 billion.[50] Under his plan, the Sunshine State would completely eliminate its corporate income tax by 2018. The governor is laser focused on job creation; he is looking to fulfill his promise to create 700,000 jobs in that time frame. As Robert McClure, president of the James Madison Institute in Tallahassee, put it, Gov. Scott's budget gives "an opportunity for American ingenuity and the free market to flourish."[51]

Some dedicated class warriors will angrily attack proponents of these business friendly, pro-growth tax measures. However, as we have said for years, businesses do not pay taxes, people do, and economists from all parts of the political spectrum agree. Don't take our word for it—even the left leaning Tax Policy Center Blog recently admitted that states need to rid themselves of corporate income taxes: "State corporate income taxes are lineal descendents of the federal version and share many of its flaws. They doubly tax income at the firm and individual level, penalize businesses that organize as corporations, and reward debt versus equity finance. They also are very sensitive to the business cycle, and tend to plunge when the economy sags."[52] Well said.

Our guess is that many other states will be following a competitiveness agenda as the revenue picture starts to improve. State corporate income taxes are low hanging fruit for tax reformers looking to make a bold statement and declare their states open for business.

The Wealth of States:
People (and Businesses) Vote with their Feet

We have argued in these reports that American workers, families, and businesses are repelled by high taxes, overspending, and excessive regulation. Still, many policymakers and pundits remain unconvinced. We have all heard the flawed arguments: people and businesses do not change their behavior in response to government policy. No matter how high the taxes or how onerous the regulations, people will simply grin and bear whatever weights government places on their shoulders.

Now we have powerful confirmation of the impact that bad state economic policies have on the vitality of states. This confirmation comes from one of the most unimpeachable of sources: the U.S. census. The new 2010 census data tracks population trends among the 50 states. These numbers tell us a significant amount of information about which states and regions are prospering and which are suffering from economic decline. This new data confirms an unmistakable migration pattern over the past decade: the higher the taxes and the tighter the government choke-hold on a state economy, the more likely people are to pack up their bags and leave—or for those outside the state, to stay away. For the states who have continued to neglect competitiveness over this decade, the 2010 census results show that it is time for them to pay the piper for their anti-growth policymaking.

As Figure 2 illustrates, the big winners over the past decade are clear: Texas and Florida were the only two states to gain multiple new congressional seats. However, with an incredible gain of four seats in the last 10 years, Texas had twice the population gain of Florida and certainly has a

legitimate claim to bragging rights for its exceptional performance. On the other side of the equation, only two states lost more than one congressional seat: Both high tax New York and Ohio will each have two fewer members of Congress and two fewer electoral votes as a result.

America's New Rust Belt: The Northeast

America's Rust Belt region, which used to be confined mostly to the liberal upper Midwest, now extends to virtually every state in the Northeast. With the exception of Delaware, every one of the 20 states north of the Mason-Dixon Line from Minnesota to Maine had below average population growth.[53] The Northeast is looking more like

TABLE 2 | **State Winners and Losers 2000-2010**

Top Winners	Population Change	Top Marginal Personal Income Tax Rate	2000-2009 Average State/Local Tax Burden (%)	2000-2009 Average State/Local Tax Burden ($)
Nevada	35.10%	0.00%	7.37%	$3,078.23
Arizona	24.60%	4.54%	8.78%	$2,962.07
Utah	23.80%	5.00%	9.89%	$3,103.95
Idaho	21.10%	7.80%	9.67%	$3,070.95
Texas	20.60%	0.00%	7.55%	$2,693.87
North Carolina	18.50%	7.75%	9.66%	$3,246.84
Georgia	18.30%	6.00%	9.17%	$3,157.88
Florida	17.60%	0.00%	8.64%	$3,362.07
Colorado	16.90%	4.63%	8.56%	$3,675.74
South Carolina	15.30%	7.00%	8.54%	$2,626.56
Average	**21.18%**	**4.27%**	**8.78%**	**$3,097.82**
Top Losers	Population Change	Top Marginal Personal Income Tax Rate	2000-2009 Average State/Local Tax Burden (%)	2000-2009 Average State/Local Tax Burden ($)
Pennsylvania	3.40%	7.05%	10.06%	$3,717.86
Illinois	3.30%	5.00%	9.48%	$3,893.67
Massachusetts	3.10%	5.30%	9.99%	$4,779.85
Vermont	2.80%	8.95%	10.19%	$3,714.94
West Virginia	2.50%	6.50%	9.28%	$2,544.09
New York	2.10%	12.62%	11.88%	$5,245.37
Ohio	1.60%	7.93%	10.11%	$3,482.77
Louisiana	1.40%	3.90%	8.30%	$2,554.47
Rhode Island	0.40%	5.99%	10.81%	$4,142.37
Michigan	-0.60%	6.85%	9.45%	$3,277.07
Average	**2.00%**	**7.01%**	**9.95%**	**$3,735.24**

* All tax rates and burdens are state and local if applicable.
Source: U.S. Census Bureau, Laffer Associates, Tax Foundation

the economically moribund continent of Europe. Meanwhile, as Table 2 shows, the booming states in the Mountain West and South have been busy racing to the top, fortifying their economic and political clout over the last decade.

So we asked the key question: has our annual ranking of the economic outlook based on 15 policy variables for the states matched the population trends of the 50 states? Absolutely. The census migration patterns confirm that, at least over the past decade, anti-growth economic policies repel people while low tax and limited government policies attract them. The 10 states with the highest population gains increased their resident populations by more than 21 percent, while the states with the lowest gains grew at only one-tenth that pace, by 2 percent.[54] That is an enormous difference.

Over the past decade, the 10 biggest population gainers had an average state and local tax burden of $3,098. The average for the 10 states with the lowest population gain was $3,735—more than 20 percent greater. The average top personal income tax rate in the 10 fastest growing states was just more than 4 percent versus more than 7 percent in the 10 slowest growing states. Clearly, states with the steepest tax rates, poor labor policy, excessive levels of government spending and hiring, overregulation of business, and tort laws that encourage frivolous lawsuits end up chasing jobs, businesses, and families to other states. In contrast, low tax states were magnets for new residents (see Table 2).[55]

The new numbers released from the U.S. Census Bureau reveal the full extent to which America has become a nation of literal movers and shakers. Our friend Richard Vedder calculates that "all told, 4,274,072 more persons moved out of the 10 states with the highest state and local tax burden (as a percent of personal income) than moved in. Put differently, every day on average—weekends and holidays included—1,265 persons left the high tax states, nearly one a minute."[56] Figure 3 on page 12 shows the states that have lost the most congressional seats over the past 50 years.

The migration pattern from the high cost states to competitive states is not a new phenomenon. Over the past decades, tens of millions of Americans have voted with their feet against anti-growth policies that reduce economic freedom and opportunity in states mostly located in the Northeast and Midwest.

This decline in population—and influence—is not a new occurrence for these states at the bottom. What is new in this census count is not nearly as intuitive. California, a state we have repeatedly castigated for poor policymaking in past editions of this publication, witnessed a historic first in this census. For the first time since becoming a state in 1850, the Golden State will not gain a congressional seat through reapportionment.[57]

As it turns out, liberalism's laboratory is not as popular as some on the Left would have you believe. How a state with Silicon Valley, great research institutions, not to mention the beaches of Santa Barbara, Big Sur, and La Jolla can be falling

Figure 2 | Apportionment of the U.S. House of Representatives Based on the 2010 Census

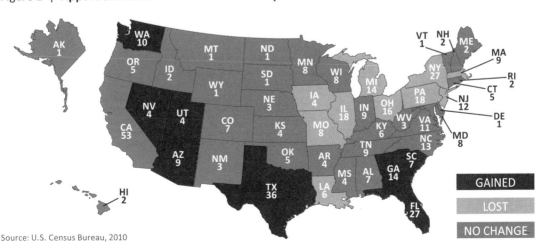

Source: U.S. Census Bureau, 2010

Figure 3 | **States with Largest Net Loss of Congressional Seats Since 1960**

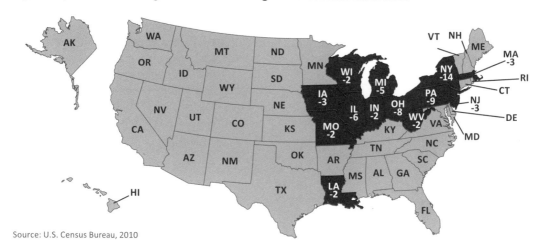

Source: U.S. Census Bureau, 2010

behind in population growth is a true testament to the consequences of anti-growth policies.[58]

The big winners in this interstate competition for jobs and growth have generally been the states in the South and West, such as Texas, Tennessee, Georgia, and Florida. The big losers have been in the Rust Belt regions of the Midwest. The demoralizing symptoms of economic despair in states like Michigan, Ohio, and Illinois include lost population, falling housing values, a shrinking tax base, business out-migration, capital flight, high unemployment rates, and less money for schools, roads, and aging infrastructure.

Escape from Detroit

In an announcement that shocked even those most attuned to the horrific problems facing Detroit, the U.S. Census Bureau recently reported that the Motor City has suffered a population loss of 25 percent in just the past 10 years, and now approximately only 700,000 people call Motown home.[59] That is hardly enough for one congressional seat! It is hard to believe Detroit was home to nearly 2 million residents in 1950.[60]

While the city's official unemployment rate hovers at a Great Depression level of 28 percent, there is recent evidence that fewer than 37 percent of Detroit's residents are actually working.[61] Little wonder that the city of Detroit recently announced plans to demolish 10,000 abandoned properties.[62] This is just another big failure for big government.

Even worse for this laboratory of liberalism, a recent survey conducted by Detroit Regional News Hub and Intellitrends shows that one in three metro Detroit residents would like to leave.[63] And why should they not? The city charges residents a 2.5 percent city income tax for the privilege of living within city limits.[64] But that is not all: The revenue hungry city government actually imposes a tax on nonresidents who work in the city. In what is one of the worst ideas we can think of, the city levies a 1 percent corporate income tax for businesses located in the city. Did anyone ever tell the city's policymakers capital is mobile? Of course it is very easy for capital to move between states, but it is even easier for profitable enterprises to avoid predatory local taxes.

Unsurprisingly, only 14 percent of residents in the Regional News Hub-Intellitrends survey "see the region as a good place to do business." Alas, Motown's anti-business philosophy has been ingrained for years. The "progressives" who have run the city government for decades are more concerned about preserving big government than about reigning in the costs of doing business within their borders.

The massive loss of jobs and human capital from this once great American city is truly appalling and should serve as a warning to states and cities across the country: Do not repeat the mistakes of the Motor City. David Littman, former chief economist at Comerica Bank (a company formerly headquartered in Detroit), says of

Figure 4 | **Right-to-Work States**

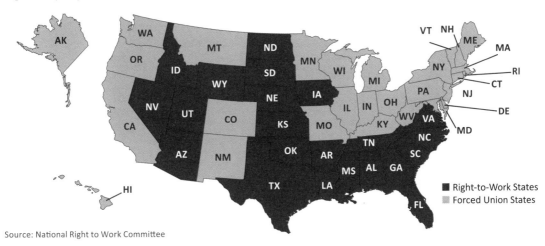

Source: National Right to Work Committee

Detroit, "It can't be stated more clearly: It's time to wake up, face economic reality, and reform."[65]

More Failures of "Progressive" Policy

It must be infuriating for progressives in states like Connecticut, Massachusetts, New Jersey, and New York to learn that their states are attracting fewer new people than those they have long ridiculed as backwaters, such as Alabama and Arkansas. In fact, Massachusetts, New York, and Rhode Island had less population growth than the nation's poorest state, Mississippi.

But doesn't the nicer weather, rather than tax policy, mostly explain these variations? Without question weather matters, and states with milder climates are doing better as Northeast and Midwest snowbirds traverse to the South and West. But weather does not come close to explaining everything. Even if we look within regions of the country, we see differences in economic outcomes weather cannot explain. For example, California has long been the jewel of the West Coast, but it has raised taxes and imposed ever more stringent environmental and workplace regulations. It ranked second to last in population growth of the 12 westernmost states, ahead only of Montana. If California is the model for how not to run a state, as we outlined in last year's edition of this publication, many governors are looking at Texas, which has led the nation in job growth over the past three years, as the state with the best policy to emulate. Alaska may have the worst climate

in the country and Hawaii arguably has the best, but Alaska had slightly faster population growth than Hawaii over the last decade. It is amazing, but true.

Here is one explanation of why people and businesses choose some states over others: Of the nine states with no income tax, seven had above average population growth while only two, New Hampshire and South Dakota, were below the average. Nevada, Texas, and Florida—each of which has no income tax—all ranked in the top eight in migration. The other five fastest growing states had very low overall tax burdens. New Hampshire's population growth rate was only 6.5 percent, but that was by far the highest in New England and more than double the rate of growth of its sister state, Vermont, which has one of the highest income taxes.

Wealthy people are not the only ones repelled by high taxes. People move to where the jobs are. Which states are those? One variable we have used on our economic competitiveness model is right-to-work laws.[66] We have posited that people and businesses want to move to places where workers have the freedom to decide whether they would like to join a union. According to an analysis by the National Right to Work Foundation, people were much more attracted to right-to-work than forced union states. From 2000 to 2010, right-to-work states' aggregate population increased by 15.5 percent (from 107.61 million to 124.29 million), while forced union states' aggregate population increased by 6.1 percent (from 173.24 million to 183.75 million).[67] That amounts to two and a half times faster growth for states allowing workers the right to decide for themselves whether they want to join a union.[68]

When we look at the age of movers, we see that, indeed, the working age population is most influenced by right-to-work laws. From 1998 to 2008 (the most recent period for which we have age specific state population data), the population of 25–34 year olds in right-to-work states increased by 16.0 percent (from 14.361 million to 16.654 million), while the population in that age bracket for forced union states fell by 0.6 percent (from 24.32 million to 24.17 million). Right-to-work states attract the most productive members of society. That young adults are overrepresented in the net migration indicates that jobs, not lifestyle considerations, are the principal factor in the movement from forced union states.

What can we deduce from all of this? Policies do have consequences. We live in a world that is in competition—for capital, jobs, and brainpower. States are not just competing against each other, but they are competing against China, India, Indonesia, Europe, and many other places eager to attract businesses and jobs. That President Barack Obama, on the national level, is pushing tax and regulatory policies making the United States less competitive globally is all the more reason for states to get their policies aligned with growth. As George Buckley, CEO of 3M, said recently, "Politicians forget that business has choice. We're not indentured servants and we will do business where it's good and friendly. If it's hostile, incrementally, things will slip away. We've got a real choice between manufacturing in Canada and Mexico—which tend to be pro-business—or America."[69]

Beware of the Class Warriors

There is a lot of talk in Washington and state capitals about how to promote equity and tax fairness. Figure 5 shows that the rich do pay their fair share in federal taxes. The top 1 percent of earners nearly pays a larger share of federal income taxes than the bottom 95 percent. This happened for the first time in American history in 2007, even after tax rates were cut under President George W. Bush.

Some critics argue that the rich pay most of the taxes because they make most of the income.

Figure 5 | Top 1 Percent Pays Nearly as Much as Bottom 95 Percent Combined

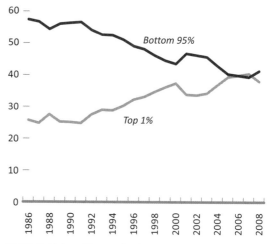

Source: U.S. Internal Revenue Service

Indeed, the top 1 percent of earners makes about 25 percent of income, but their share of the federal income tax is much higher than their share of earned income. It is also worth noting that the bottom 50 percent of Americans now pays less than 3 percent of the total federal income tax.[70] The U.S. tax system is highly progressive already. Further, increasing tax rates may cause the rich to pay a smaller share of taxes—the opposite of the intended result.[71]

Class warfare is, alas, still a common theme in state capitals around the country, and tax hikes aimed at the rich are in vogue with some left-wing legislators. We have seen a record number of states consider or enact tax increases on the rich in recent years. These "millionaires taxes" levied on residents in the highest state tax brackets were all enacted in states with politically liberal dominated legislatures. In each case, *Stateline* reports, "Democrats muscled through the tax rate increases, arguing that wealthier residents can afford a higher share of the tax burden—particularly in a recession."[72] In Hawaii, which along with Oregon now shares the highest state income tax in America (11 percent), advocates of the big tax hike on the rich enacted in Honolulu usually explain the rationale for it in terms of class warfare. The tax hike targeted toward these rich is hardly going to help rebalance the worst real estate crisis in decades in Hawaii.

We doubt the tax hikes aimed at the wealthiest

residents are done. With deficits that may surpass $100 billion in the states for fiscal year 2012, we expect big pushes for tax increases in Connecticut, Minnesota, and yet again Maryland, California, and Hawaii. It is a good bet that liberal legislatures will continue to try to raise rates on businesses and high income residents.

Class warriors often forget that many of these high income earners are actually small businesses, which, through subchapter S Corporations (S Corps), Limited Liability Partnerships (LLPs), and other "pass-through" entities, pay their taxes through the individual side of the tax code. In fact, these small businesses make up more than 90 percent of all businesses, employ more than 50 percent of American workers, and pay more than 40 percent of all business taxes.[73] Millionaires taxes are often paid by small business owners and operators, making these misguided policies job killers, plain and simple.

More troubling for the class warriors is the very real possibility that millionaires taxes will shift behavior and drive capital to more hospitable states and then suffer the Laffer Curve effect of revenue losses. We will explain later in greater detail why this approach is likely to be a failure in raising revenues and in helping a state economy. For now, we point out that one state that raised tax rates on millionaires in 2008, Maryland, already witnessed a 33 percent decline in tax returns from millionaire households, according to the *Washington Examiner*.[74] Predictably, many misguided, left leaning pundits were quick to point out that this loss of millionaires was simply caused by the recession. However, a Bank of America-Merrill Lynch study of federal tax return data on people who migrated from one state to another found that Maryland lost $1 billion of its net tax base in 2008 by residents moving to other states.[75] The rich have literally disappeared from the state tax collector's sights.

State lawmakers almost always overestimate the popularity of tax hikes on the rich. Former governor Jon Corzine of New Jersey was defeated after raising tax rates on the rich twice.[76] New Jersey voters were angry at the way Mr. Corzine had failed to create jobs, failed to balance the budget, and failed to ease the highest property tax burden in the nation.[77] Thankfully, Chris Christie, his successor, who has emerged as a conservative star in the deficit plagued Garden State, vetoed a giant tax increase less than 30 minutes after the legislature passed it.[78] He was cheered by voters and businesses across the state.

We hate to keep picking on California, New Jersey, and New York, but they continue to be models of how not to govern a state—though Gov. Christie is heroically trying to turn things around in New Jersey and Gov. Cuomo has so far impressed us with his stance on fiscal discipline in the Empire State. These three states impose tax rates at or near the highest in the nation and about twice the national average.

New York City mayor Michael Bloomberg once called Manhattan a "luxury good," meaning that people are willing to pay a premium to live there. The pols in Sacramento say much of the same thing about living in the Golden State. But what these jurisdictions are discovering is that there are limits. The rich will pay more to live in Santa Barbara or Manhattan penthouses for sure, but not hundreds of thousands or even millions of dollars more—compared to the tax savings of living and running their business in Austin, Palm Beach, Nashville, Seattle, or countless other cities in states where there is no income tax at all. And, again, when the rich escape, they often take more than their own direct tax payments. They also take their businesses and jobs with them. That is the collateral damage high tax rates have on the middle class and poor.

The result of these high tax rates has not been to balance state budgets or improve the financing of vital state services. Far from it. You cannot balance the budget on the backs of 1 percent of the most productive citizens of a state. They will leave, and as the 2010 census points out, they are leaving. The goal should be to bring them back, not drive them away.

Illinois and Oregon Repeat Maryland's Folly

Lawmakers in Illinois have easily won the award for the worst tax policies enacted so far in 2011. Shortly after the New Year, during the night (rushing to pass the tax before the new legislature was sworn into office), Gov. Pat Quinn got his New Year's wish to hike personal and corporate income tax rates. As a result of this largest tax increase in Illinois history, individuals in the Land of Lincoln will now pay an income tax rate 67 percent higher than last year's, and corporations will see their tax rates increase by 50 percent.[79]

In the state that gave us the great Ronald Reagan, it is so disappointing to see that a majority of the current politicians in Springfield are so willing to ignore the consequences of such a major tax increase. Unfortunately for the workers of Illinois, many job creators cannot ignore such a large cost increase. As Doug Oberhelman, CEO of Caterpillar, said, "I want to stay here, but as the leader of this business, I have to do what's right for Caterpillar when making decisions about where to invest. The direction that this state is headed in is not favorable to business, and I'd like to work with you to change that."[80]

After Gov. Quinn signed the job killing tax increase into law, Steve Stanek called Illinois, the "Land of Larceny" in a *New York Post* column.[81] Governors from Scott Walker in Wisconsin to Chris Christie of New Jersey and Mitch Daniels of Indiana were busy sending welcome letters to Illinois businesses, explaining the benefits of relocating to their state.[82] As the *Chicago Tribune* put it, "Too bad Mitch Daniels governs Indiana, not Illinois."[83] The tax increase was so unpopular even Mayor Richard M. Daley blasted it.[84]

Illinois is, undoubtedly, in tough financial shape today. The state has a higher default risk than Iceland and is currently approaching that of Iraq.[85] Furthermore, as discussed earlier in this chapter, the state's pension system is in full financial meltdown. To be sure, the Land of Lincoln faced rough financial straits before the current tax hike, but the low rate income tax was one of the state's last remaining vestiges of pro-growth tax policy. Now that the lid has been blown off the income tax, we expect Illinois to gradually drift toward the dangerous category of California and New York.

In 2009, the Oregon Legislature raised the tax rate to 10.8 percent on those with family incomes of $250,000 and to 11 percent on income above $500,000—this gives Oregon the dubious distinction of being tied (with Hawaii) for the highest personal income taxes in the nation.[86] Voters ratified the tax increase on individuals and another on businesses in January 2010, but now the state treasury admits it is collecting far less revenue than the bean counters projected. The Portland *Register-Guard* reports that after the tax was raised, "income tax and other revenue collections began plunging so steeply that any gains from the two measures seemed trivial."[87] Paul Warner,

head of the state's Legislative Revenue Office, said, "We're thinking we're right around half of what we expected about this time."[88] One reason revenues are so low is that nearly one-quarter of the rich tax filers seem to have gone missing. The state expected 38,000 Oregonians to pay the higher tax, but only 28,000 did.[89] Funny how that always happens. On those missing returns, the Oregon State treasury collects a full 11 percent . . . of nothing.

During the debate, an academic study by the state's free market Cascade Policy Institute warned of the economic harm that the tax increases would cause.[90] The political left ridiculed the study, but as the state has now suffered from the predicted economic malaise, Steve Buckstein, Cascade's founder, says, this is a "told you so" story.[91]

The tax was not enacted until June of 2009, but it was retroactively applied to earnings dating back to January 1, 2009. For the first half of the year, wealthy Oregon residents were unable to take steps to avoid the tax ambush because they did not see it coming. This epitomizes bad tax policy. One of Oregon's most notable job creators, Nike's Phil Knight, spoke out during the debate over the misguided tax hike. He warned Oregonians that the tax increases were "anti-business, anti-success, anti-inspirational, anti-humanitarian, and most ironically, in the long run, they will deprive the state of tax revenue, not increase it."[92]

The big revenue loss from tax mitigation strategies will show up on tax return data in 2010 and 2011. The biggest loss of revenues came from capital gains receipts. The new 11 percent top tax rate applies to stock and asset sales, which means Oregonians now pay virtually the highest capital gains tax in North America. Instead of $3.5 billion of capital gains in 2009, Oregon had only $2 billion to tax—a shocking 43 percent less than expected.[93] Successful people like Nike owner Phil Knight do not get rich by being fools with their money; they do not sell tens of millions of dollars in assets when capital gains taxes go up.

The tax increase defenders in the Salem legislature keep insisting the new levies have not affected business decisions or the state's economy—which is underperforming and includes an unemployment rate that has risen to 10 percent. These same lawmakers who say taxes do not matter are arranging sweetheart income and property tax write-offs for giant firms so they do not have to pay the sky high taxes everyone else does. And these are the people who preach tax fairness?

Count us as not surprised by any of this since it is all an instant replay of what happened in Maryland and other states that have unsuccessfully attempted to enrich the treasury by taxing millionaires. "This is a temporary thing," argues Phil Barnhart, Oregon's House Revenue Committee chairman. He predicts taxes "will be back up."[94] Perhaps, but that is what the politicos in California and New York have been praying for year after year as their states sink deeper into an abyss of debt. Oregonians were suckered into believing they could balance their budget on the backs of business owners and the wealthy. They should repeal the tax hike mishap before it does more harm. In the meantime, if state officials want to find the millionaires, they might want to start the search in Texas, the state that leads the nation in job creation and has an income tax 11 percentage points lower than Oregon's.

Oregon is tied with Hawaii now with the highest state income tax rate in the nation. Hawaii's income tax was raised several years ago to balance the budget there. However, the Aloha State still reports hefty budget deficits. We have seen this movie before. How many times do we have to tell and retell this story before the politicians finally get it? The politicians in Oregon and Illinois chose to ignore the well-documented failures of past income tax increase. Unfortunately for them, the laws of competitiveness, or economics 101 for that matter, cannot be as easily ignored.

The ALEC-Laffer State Economic Competitiveness Model

Of course, every state aspires to be a high octane, high growth state—a destination, not a place where people say with nostalgia that they are "from." The economic performance ratings in our final chapter did not just happen by chance. It is not a random occurrence that people move from Michigan to Florida or from California to Texas.

Table 3 | ALEC-Laffer State Economic Outlook Rankings, 2011

Overall Economic Outlook Rank			
1	Utah	26	North Carolina
2	South Dakota	27	Kansas
3	Virginia	28	New Hampshire
4	Wyoming	29	Alaska
5	Idaho	30	Wisconsin
6	Colorado	31	West Virginia
7	North Dakota	32	Nebraska
8	Tennessee	33	Washington
9	Missouri	34	Delaware
10	Florida	35	Connecticut
11	Georgia	36	Montana
12	Arizona	37	Minnesota
13	Arkansas	38	Ohio
14	Oklahoma	39	New Mexico
15	Louisiana	40	Kentucky
16	Indiana	41	Pennsylvania
17	Nevada	42	Rhode Island
18	Texas	43	Oregon
19	Mississippi	44	Illinois
20	Alabama	45	New Jersey
21	Maryland	46	Hawaii
22	South Carolina	47	California
23	Iowa	48	Maine
24	Massachusetts	49	Vermont
25	Michigan	50	New York

They are driven by the law of supply and demand: High growth states supply jobs, high incomes, and opportunities that Americans demand.

In this publication, we investigate what policy levers state legislators control that can make their state a desirable location. Many of the most important factors that make a place attractive—such as the climate or accessibility to beautiful beaches or mountains or the mineral resources in the ground—are, of course, beyond politicians' control. No one should think Gary, Ind. will ever compete on equal footing with Malibu, Calif., or that Trenton, N.J. will ever be as desirable a destination as Hilton Head, S.C.

The central premise of this publication is that the state economic policy decisions made by state legislators do not matter just in terms of how a state performs financially; they matter much more than that. State officials can influence these factors, that is, the economic and fiscal policies that contribute to—or in all too many cases against—the livability of a state.

In this study, we have identified 15 policy variables that have a proven impact on the migration of capital—both investment capital and human capital—into and out of states. They are the basic ingredients to our 2011 State Economic Competitiveness Rankings. Each of these 15 factors is influenced directly by state lawmakers through the legislative process. Generally speaking, states that spend less—especially on income-transfer programs—and states that tax less—particularly on productive activities such as working or investing—experience higher growth rates than states that tax and spend more. The 15 factors are as follows:

- Highest Marginal Personal Income Tax Rate
- Highest Marginal Corporate Income Tax Rate
- Personal Income Tax Progressivity

- Property Tax Burden
- Sales Tax Burden
- Tax Burden from all Remaining Taxes
- Estate Tax or Inheritance Tax (Yes or No)
- Recent Tax Policy Changes 2009–10
- Debt Service as a Share of Tax Revenue
- Public Employees (Per 10,000 Residents)
- Quality of a State's Legal System
- State Minimum Wage
- Workers' Compensation Costs
- Right-to-Work State (Yes or No)
- Number of Tax or Expenditure Limits

Based on these 15 policy factors, we present to you the 2011 ALEC-Laffer State Economic Competitiveness Index rankings of each state's economic outlook (see Chapter 4).

Conclusion

The conclusion is getting to be nearly inescapable that states with high and rising tax burdens are more likely to suffer in an economic decline while those with lower and falling tax burdens are more likely to enjoy robust economic growth. Here is a quick synopsis of the results:

- The overall level of taxation has an inverse relationship to economic growth in a state.
- The change in the level and rate of taxation impacts state economic performance.
- High tax rates are especially harmful.
- Some state taxes have a more negative impact than others.

Balancing state budgets and bringing jobs and employers back to the states in a national environment with unemployment rates exceeding 9 percent will be the top two priorities of governors and legislators in 2011. This publication will serve as a roadmap for how to make that happen.

ENDNOTES

1 Interview with the authors.

2 Mitchell, Matthew. "State Spending Restraint: An Analysis of the Path Not Taken." The Mercatus Center at George Mason University. August 17, 2010.

3 Mitchell, Matthew. "State Budget Gaps and State Budget Growth." The Mercatus Center at George Mason University. August 2, 2010.

4 Ibid.

5 Malanga, Steven. "Anti-Business States Awash in Red Ink." Real Clear Markets. August 6, 2008.

6 Gilroy, Leonard and Williams, Jonathan, et al. State Budget Reform Toolkit. American Legislative Exchange Council, 2011. See also, Mitchell, Matthew. "State Budget Gaps and State Budget Growth." The Mercatus Center at George Mason University. August 2, 2010.

7 "75 Percent Blame State Budget Problems on Politicians' Unwillingness to Cut Spending." Rasmussen Reports. July 8, 2010.

8 Laffer, Arthur B., Moore, Stephen and Williams. Jonathan. Rich States, Poor States, 3rd ed. American Legislative Exchange Council. 2010. See also, Hough, Michael and Williams, Jonathan. "Congress Crafting a Stimulus to Nowhere." Washington Examiner. February 5, 2009.

9 Dougherty, Conor. "State Tax Collections Tick Up." The Wall Street Journal. April 19, 2011.

10 Dadayan, Lucy, and Boyd, Donald. "State Tax Revenues Gained Strength in 2010, Following Deep Declines." The Nelson A. Rockefeller Institute of Government: State Revenue Report, no. 82. February 2011.

11 Ibid.

12 U.S. Government Accountability Office. "Report to the Ranking Member, Committee on the Budget, House of Representatives. State and Local Governments: Fiscal Pressures Could Have Implications for Future Delivery of Intergovernmental Programs." July 2010.

13 National Governors Association. "The Big Reset: State Government after the Great Recession." February 23, 2010.

14 Leonard, Bryan. "Just How Big Are Public Pension Liabilities?" State Budget Solutions. March 4, 2011.

15 Elmendorf, Douglas. "Fiscal Stress Faced by Local Governments." Congressional Budget Office. December 2010.

16 Brown, Willie. "Homeland Security Chief Takes Responsibility." San Francisco Chronicle. January 3, 2010.

17 Malanga, Steve. "How States Hide Their Budget Deficits." The Wall Street Journal. August 23, 2010.

18 Gilroy, Leonard and Williams, Jonathan, et al. State Budget Reform Toolkit. American Legislative Exchange Council. 2011.

19 Williams, Bob. "Performance-Based Budgeting." Inside ALEC. April 2009.

20 Bureau of Labor Statistics. U.S. Department of Labor. News Release. March 9, 2011.

21 Barro, Josh. "The False Obstacles to Pension Reform." Real Clear Markets. October 5, 2010.

22 Ibid.

23 Henninger, Daniel. "Taxes: A Defining Issue." The Wall Street Journal. July 29, 2010.

24 Davis, Aaron, and Marimow, Ann. "Md. Teacher's Union Floats Alternative Pension Plan." Washington Post. March 23, 2011.

25 Biggs, Andrew. "The Market Value of Public-Sector Pension Deficits." American Enterprise Institute. April 2010. See also, "State Pensions and Retiree Healthcare Benefits: The Trillion Dollar Gap." PEW Center on the States. February 18, 2010; and Novy-Marx, Robert and Rauh, Joshua. "Public Pension Promises: How Big Are They and What Are They Worth." Journal of Finance. October 8, 2010.

26 Keefe, John. "Current Accounting Rules Understate Pension Problem." Institutional Investor. February 16, 2011.

27 Summers, Adam. "Warren Buffett on Public Pensions." Reason Foundation. March 26, 2011.

28 Guth, Robert and Corkery, Michael. "Gates Says Benefits Costs Hit Schools." The Wall Street Journal. March 3, 2011.

29 Cooper, Michael, and Walsh, Mary Williams. "Public Pensions, Once Off Limits, Face Budget Cuts." The New York Times. April 25, 2011.

30 MacDonald, Elizabeth. "States Increasingly Turn to 401ks to Replace Pensions." Fox Business. April 5, 2011.

31 Liljenquist, Dan. Testimony before the U.S. House Committee on Oversight and Government Reform. March 15, 2011.

32 "33% Renewables Portfolio Standard Implementation Analysis Preliminary Results." California Public Utilities Commission. June 2009.

33 "How Less Became More: Wind, Power and Unintended Consequences in the Colorado Energy Market." BENTEK Energy, LLC. April 16, 2010.

34 Watkins, Bob. "If California Is Doing So Great, Why Are So Many Leaving?" Fox and Hounds Daily. December 14, 2010.

35 California's Legislative Analyst's Office. Letter to Assembly Member Dan Logue. May 13, 2010.

36 *Ibid.*

37 *Ibid.*

38 Laffer, Arthur B., Moore, Stephen and Williams, Jonathan. *Rich States, Poor States*, 3rd ed. American Legislative Exchange Council. 2010.

39 "Governor Ends a Nearly Century Old Tax on Missouri Business by Signing Missouri Chamber Priority into Law." Missouri Chamber of Commerce and Industry. Press Release. April 26, 2011.

40 Moritz, Rob. "Senate Panel Rejects House Capital Gains Tax Cut Proposal." *Arkansas News.* March 16, 2011.

41 Hertneky, Dana. "Oklahoma Lawmaker Wants to Eliminate State's Personal Income Tax." *News 9.* January 6, 2011.

42 "Oklahoma Senate Approves Income Tax Abolishment Plan." *Associated Press.* March 3, 2011.

43 Whitten, Rachel. "House Votes No on Sales Tax Repeal." *Kansas Reporter.* March 17, 2011.

44 Hamilton, Amy. "North Dakota House Rejects Governor's Tax Cut in Favor of Larger One." *Tax Analysts.* April 6, 2011.

45 Setz, Karen. "Iowa House Approves Income Tax Cut." *Tax Analysts.* February 18, 2011.

46 Upmeyer, Linda. "20 Percent Income Tax Cut for All Iowans" Press Release. February 17, 2011.

47 Hanel, Joe. "Arizona Enacts Corporate Tax Cut, Single Sales Factor." *Tax Analysts.* February 22, 2011.

48 Atkins, Chris, and Williams, Jonathan. "Tax Reform in Michigan: Replacing the Single Business Tax." Tax Foundation Special Report, no. 149. January 2007.

49 Lohrmann, Niki. "Indiana Lawmakers Approve Corporate Tax Cut." *Tax Analysts.* May 3, 2011.

50 Follick, Joe. "Florida Governor's Budget Proposes $8 Billion in Spending and Tax Cuts." *Tax Analysts.* February 8, 2011.

51 Clendinen, Tanja. "Florida Governor Strives to Cut Taxes, Spending." *Budget and Tax News.* April 2011.

52 Gordon, Tracy. "Take the State Corporate Income Tax . . . Please!" TaxVox: The Tax Policy Center Blog. May 14, 2010.

53 U.S. Census Bureau. "Population Distribution and Change: 2000 to 2010." March 2011.

54 *Ibid.*

55 Barone, Michael. "The Eyes of Texas Are Sparkling in the 2010 Census." *Real Clear Politics.* March 28, 2011.

56 Vedder, Richard. "High Tax Burdens Lead to Population Losses." *Inside ALEC.* April 2010.

57 Rove, Karl. "The GOP Targets State Legislatures." *The Wall Street Journal.* March 4, 2010.

58 Steel, Michelle. "Lessons from Liberalism's Laboratory: California." *Inside ALEC.* April 2010.

59 "Census: Detroit's Population Plummets 25 Percent." *NBC News.* March 22, 2011.

60 "Detroit's Population Drops to Lowest Level in 100 Years." *Reuters.* March 23, 2011.

61 Cooper, Michael, and Walsh, Mary Williams. "Public Pensions, Once Off Limits, Face Budget Cuts." *The New York Times.* April 25, 2011.

62 Kellogg, Alex P. "Detroit Shrinks Itself, Historic Homes and All." *The Wall Street Journal.* May 14, 2010.

63 Oosting, Jonathan. "Study: Young People Hopeful for Metro Detroit, but 1 in 3 Residents Want to Leave." MLive.com. April 21, 2010.

64 City of Detroit. Finance Department.

65 Littman, David. "The Economics of Decay." *D Business Magazine.* July–August 2009.

66 Vedder, Richard, Denhart, Matthew, and Robe, Jonathan. "Right-to-Work and Indiana's Economic Future." Indiana Chamber of Commerce Foundation. January 2011.

67 Barone, Michael. "The Eyes of Texas Are Sparkling in the 2010 Census." *Real Clear Politics.* March 28, 2011.

68 "Right to Work States Benefit From Faster Growth, Higher Real Purchasing Power- 2010 Update." National Institute for Labor Relations Research. November 2010.

69 "3M CEO Blasts Obama as Anti-business." *Reuters.* February 27, 2011.

70 Robyn, Mark and Prante, Gerald. "Summary of the Latest Federal Individual Income Tax Data." The Tax Foundation. October 6, 2010.

71 Laffer, Arthur. "The Soak-the-Rich Catch-22." *The Wall Street Journal.* August 2, 2010.

72 Gramlich, John. "State Tax Hikes Take Aim at Top Earners." *Stateline.* September 2, 2009.

73 Carroll, Robert. "Testimony before the Committee on Ways and Means Subcommittee on Select Revenue Measures." U.S. House of Representatives. March 3, 2011.

74 Fabel, Leah. "Millionaires Flee Maryland Taxes." *Washington Examiner.* May 27, 2009.

75 "Maryland's Mobile Millionaires." *The Wall Street Journal.* March 12, 2009.

76 "Taxpayer Group Calls on Corzine to Denounce Assembly Democrat Tax Increase." Americans for Tax Reform. June 29, 2005. See also, Hladky, Gregory B. "Tax Increase Certain." *New Haven Register.* February 12, 2007; and Dubay, Curtis.

"Significant Tax Increase for Pennsylvania." Tax Foundation. February 2007.

77 Malanga, Steven. "The Mob That Whacked Jersey: How Rapacious Government Withered the Garden State." *City Journal*. Spring 2006.

78 Freidman, Matt, and Fleisher, Lisa. "N.J. Gov. Chris Christie Swiftly Vetoes 'Millionaires Tax,' Property Tax Rebate Bills." *Statehouse Bureau*. May 20, 2010.

79 "Fact Finder: 2011 Tax Hike Is the Largest in Illinois History." Illinois Policy Institute. Budget and Tax Brief. April 15, 2011.

80 "Will Taxes Force Caterpillar to Leave Illinois?" *Wisconsin Ag Connection*. April 18, 2011.

81 Stanek, Steve. "Land of Larceny." *New York Post*. January 12, 2011.

82 "Gov. Christie to Launch Campaign Encouraging Illinois Businesses to Relocate to NJ." *Associated Press*. January 24, 2011.

83 "Put Illinois to Work." *Chicago Tribune*. October 19, 2010.

84 "Neighboring States, Mayor Daley Slam Illinois Tax Increase's Business Impact." *Fox Chicago News*. January 13, 2011.

85 Costin, Brian. "Illinois a Higher Default Risk than Iceland, Approaching Iraq." Illinois Policy Institute. July 16, 2010.

86 "Ducking Higher Taxes." Revenue and Outlook, *The Wall Street Journal*. December 21, 2010.

87 Steves, David. "Measure 66 Raising Less Tax Revenue Than Forecast." *Register-Guard*. December 16, 2010.

88 Esteve, Harry. "Oregon Tax Revenues from Measure 66 Coming up Short of Predictions." *The Oregonian*. August 30, 2010.

89 "Ducking Higher Taxes." Revenue and Outlook, *The Wall Street Journal*. December 21, 2010.

90 Fruits, Eric, and Pozdena, Randall. "Tax Policy and the Oregon Economy: The Effects of Measures 66 and 67." Cascade Policy Institute. December 2009.

91 Buckstein, Steve. "This Is a 'Told You So' Story about Measures 66 & 67." Cascade Policy Institute. August 26, 2010.

92 Knight, Phil. "Nike Chairman: Anti-business Climate Nurtures 66, 67." OregonLive.com. January 17, 2010.

93 "Ducking Higher Taxes." Revenue and Outlook, *The Wall Street Journal*. December 21, 2010.

94 *Ibid.*

Bellevue, Washington

State Policy Highlights and Lowlights

State Policy
Highlights and Lowlights

Framed on a wall in Arthur Laffer's office is a personal letter from Bill Gates the elder. "I am a fan of progressive taxation," he wrote. "I would say our country has prospered from using such a system—even at 70 percent rates, to say nothing of 90 percent."

It is one thing to believe in bad policy. It is quite another to push it on others. But Mr. Gates Sr.—an accomplished lawyer, now retired—and his illustrious son tried to have their way with the people of the state of Washington this past fall.

Mr. Gates Sr. personally contributed $600,000 to promote a statewide proposition on Washington's November ballot that would have imposed a brand new 5 percent tax on individuals earning over $200,000 per year and on couples earning over $400,000 per year. It would have levied an additional 4 percent surcharge on individuals and couples earning more than $500,000 and $1 million, respectively.[1]

Along with creating a new income tax on high income earners, Initiative 1098 would have reduced property, business, and occupation taxes. But creating a personal income tax was the real issue. Doing so would put any state's economy at risk.

To gauge what such a large "soak the rich" income tax would do to Washington, we need only to examine how states with the highest income-tax rates perform relative to their zero income tax counterparts. Table 4 powerfully demonstrates how high rate income taxes weaken economic performance. When you compare the nine states with the highest tax rates on earned income to the nine states with no income tax, the results speak awfully loudly for themselves.

In the past decade, the nine states with the highest personal income tax rates have, on average,

seen gross state product increase by 44.91 percent, job growth increased by 0.47 percent, and population increase 6.48 percent. In contrast, the nine states with no personal income tax—of which Washington state is one—have, on average, seen gross state product increase by 61.23 percent, job growth increased by 7.78 percent, and population increase by 13.75 percent.

The extent to which the states with the highest tax rates have underperformed those states without income taxes is shocking. Washington's past performance is especially noteworthy. However, had I-1098 passed, it would have jeopardized the competitiveness and the economic success the Evergreen State has enjoyed. And passing I-1098 would have been only the beginning. As Ohio, New Jersey, and California demonstrate, once a state adopts an income tax, there is no end to the number of reasons that tax could be extended, expanded, and increased.

Evidence of the damage income taxes cause is evident outside of the comparison between high tax and no tax states. Over the past 50 years, 11 states have introduced a state income tax exactly as Messrs. Gates and their allies proposed in Washington—and as Table 4 highlights, the consequences to state economies have been devastating.

The 11 states that adopted income taxes in the past 50 years are Connecticut (1991), New Jersey (1976), Ohio (1971), Rhode Island (1971), Pennsylvania (1971), Maine (1969), Illinois (1969), Nebraska (1967), Michigan (1967), Indiana (1963), and West Virginia (1961).[2] Each state that introduced an income tax declined as a share of total U.S. output. Some of these states—including Michigan, Pennsylvania, and Ohio—have become fiscal basket cases. As Table 5 shows, even

TABLE 4 | **The Nine States with the Lowest and Highest Marginal Personal Income Tax (PIT) Rates**
10-Year Economic Performance (1999-2009 unless otherwise noted)

State	Top PIT Rate*	Gross State Product Growth	Population Growth	Non-Farm Payroll Employment Growth	Gross State Product Per Capita Growth	Gross State Product Per Employee Growth	Total State Tax Receipts Growth**
Alaska	0.00%	80.1%	11.3%	15.03%	61.8%	59.2%	452.6%
Florida	0.00%	51.6%	15.5%	3.94%	31.3%	47.8%	82.3%
Nevada	0.00%	64.8%	31.0%	12.44%	25.9%	47.5%	100.1%
New Hampshire	0.00%	33.7%	6.8%	1.70%	25.2%	32.9%	59.6%
South Dakota	0.00%	61.5%	7.5%	7.26%	50.2%	51.2%	51.2%
Tennessee	0.00%	36.2%	10.4%	-4.28%	23.4%	41.9%	61.7%
Texas	0.00%	55.7%	18.3%	10.54%	31.6%	42.5%	75.5%
Washington	0.00%	47.6%	12.7%	3.99%	30.9%	41.9%	57.8%
Wyoming	0.00%	119.8%	10.2%	19.42%	99.4%	83.7%	172.2%
9 States with no PIT**	0.00%	61.23%	13.75%	7.78%	42.19%	49.83%	123.66%
U.S. Average**	5.68%	47.05%	8.62%	1.12%	35.62%	44.92%	70.23%
9 States with Highest Marginal PIT Rate**	9.79%	44.91%	6.48%	0.47%	36.15%	44.73%	62.43%
Delaware	8.20%	44.9%	12.6%	-1.75%	28.7%	46.2%	50.2%
Maine	8.50%	39.2%	3.2%	-0.73%	34.8%	40.8%	45.3%
Maryland	8.55%	55.1%	7.3%	3.21%	44.5%	51.0%	67.0%
Vermont	8.95%	39.3%	1.9%	0.18%	36.6%	40.0%	64.5%
New Jersey	8.97%	36.9%	3.3%	-1.84%	32.6%	40.5%	70.4%
California	10.30%	43.0%	8.7%	-2.33%	31.6%	47.2%	77.2%
Hawaii	11.00%	58.8%	6.9%	8.57%	48.5%	47.9%	72.1%
Oregon	11.00%	46.2%	11.5%	-0.59%	31.1%	46.8%	46.8%
New York	12.62%	40.8%	2.9%	-0.53%	36.9%	42.2%	68.3%

*Highest marginal state and local personal income tax rate imposed as of 1/1/11 using the tax rate of each state's largest city as a proxy for the local tax. The effect of the deductibility of federal taxes from state tax liability is included where acceptable. New Hampshire and Tennessee tax dividend and interest income only.
** Equal-weighted averages
Source: Laffer Associates

West Virginia, which was poor to begin with, became relatively poorer after adopting a state income tax.

The states with high income tax rates or that have adopted a state income tax over the past half-century have not even collected the money they hoped for. They have not avoided budget crises, nor have they provided better lives for the poor. The ongoing financial travails of California, New Jersey, Michigan, and New York all serve to demonstrate this point. That's why last year's edition of this publication devoted an entire chapter to these four states, titled "Lessons on How Not to Govern a State."

Over the past decade, tax revenue in the nine states with the highest tax rates has increased by an average of 62 percent, exactly half than in the states with no income tax. Why would Washington state want to introduce a state income tax when doing so means a less stable and less predictable source of money for state coffers?

It is easy to see why we view one of the happiest outcomes of last fall's elections to be that Washington voters trounced Initiative 1098, the

Bill Gates Sr. and government employee union financed ballot initiative to impose the state's first ever income tax. Mr. Gates and his union colleagues spent more than $6 million on the initiative to install a progressive income tax with rates as high as 9 percent on wealthy residents. High income tax states lose jobs. Just ask California, New York, and New Jersey. As *The Wall Street Journal* put it, "The absence of an income tax has been Washington's greatest comparative advantage over its high income tax neighbors in California and Oregon."[3]

This was the tax that was going to be paid, according to Mr. Gates, only by millionaires, billionaires, and gazillionaires. But a funny thing happened on the way to the voting booth: Nearly two out of three voters (65 percent) understood the Laffer Curve and rejected the "soak the rich" tax. If he wants, Mr. Gates can pay his own voluntary income tax to Washington state. Special kudos to Steve Ballmer and other Microsoft employees who supported the no income tax campaign.

As we argued in last year's edition of this publication, any state can improve its economic outlook by replacing its personal income tax with a revenue neutral—or even preferably, a net tax cut—shift to a well-designed consumption tax. Washington state was wise not to go the other direction. The Evergreen State also passed a measure to require a supermajority to raise taxes; it

TABLE 5 | Gross State Product

Relative to the United States

State	Prior to Income Tax	2009
Connecticut	1.74%	1.57%
New Jersey	3.50%	3.41%
Ohio	5.32%	3.32%
Rhode Island	0.43%	0.34%
Pennsylvania	5.64%	3.91%
Maine	0.38%	0.36%
Illinois	6.37%	4.43%
Nebraska	0.68%	0.60%
Michigan	5.12%	2.57%
Indiana	2.59%	1.84%
West Virginia	NA	0.44%

Source: U.S. Bureau of Economic Analysis

earned 65 percent of the vote. Washingtonians also voted to repeal harmful taxes on candy and sugary drinks (the "Coca-Cola tax").

We welcome the news from Washington state. In this chapter, we examine how other ballot initiatives around the country fared; the results in other states were a mixed bag.

California:
The Sun Ain't Going to Shine Anymore

While the news from Washington was positive on Election Day, we are still wondering what is wrong with California. Golden State voters opted to make California even less economically desirable by voting down a ballot initiative to suspend the state's cap-and-trade energy tax until the unemployment rate falls to 5.5 percent. With the latest statistics showing state unemployment hovering at 12 percent, the idea of postponing a new energy tax on industry, vehicles, and homeowners should have seemed the height of rationality.

Instead, liberal Silicon Valley venture capitalists teamed up with rich environmentalists to finance a fairy tale campaign claiming cap-and-trade regulations will actually increase hiring by bringing "clean energy" jobs to the state. Somehow, a majority of California voters were gullible enough to buy that. Now the state that already has nearly the highest taxes and energy bills in the country will raise these costs further, thereby putting an estimated one million manufacturing, construction, oil and gas, and transportation jobs at risk over the next decade. All this for a climate change measure even the proponents agree will do nothing to change the global temperature. Incidentally, despite the billions of dollars devoted to the "green energy" economy in California, only 1–2 percent of California jobs were green jobs in 2009.[4]

Californians also voted to eliminate the two-thirds vote requirement to pass a state budget. This looks to us like a license for the left-wing dominated legislature to borrow and spend at an even more ruinous pace. It is hard to believe this is the state that gave us Proposition 13 roughly 30 years ago.[5] It is no wonder Sacramento already has one of the worst credit ratings of the 50 states and the largest unfunded pension liabilities outside of Europe. At least fed up Californians can move to Washington state … or Tennessee.

Liberals Increase Their Dominance in the California Legislature

Until the election, passing a budget in the California Legislature required a two-thirds supermajority. This gave the Republican minority—which still holds slightly more than one-third of the seats in both the Assembly and the Senate—some say in budget matters. The requirement for a two-thirds majority usually led to the state's infamous failure to pass a budget by the June 15 deadline stipulated in the California Constitution. In 2010, the gridlock delayed passage of the fiscal 2010–11 budget by 100 days.[6]

With the passage of Proposition 25, only a simple majority is needed to pass a budget, making the process a whole new ballgame. Supposedly, a two-thirds supermajority is still required to pass tax increases. Prop. 25 read, "This measure will not change the two-thirds vote requirement for the Legislature to raise taxes." But Prop. 25's language also included this phrase: "Notwithstanding any other provision of law . . . bills providing for appropriations related to the budget may be passed [by] a majority." It is anybody's guess how that will be interpreted by the Legislature, Gov. Jerry Brown, and the courts. Thus, more uncertainty has been added to the state's business climate.

On a positive note, voters approved Prop. 26, which raises the threshold of votes in the Legislature for raising "fees" to two-thirds.[7] But if Prop. 25 is interpreted by the courts as allowing a simple majority vote for tax increases, will that cancel out Prop. 26? The uncertainty multiplies. In the past, the courts have settled conflicts between propositions based on which received a greater percentage of votes. Prop. 25 (majority vote on the budget) passed with 55 percent, but Prop. 26 (two-thirds vote for fees) passed with only 53 percent. It looks as though the major growth industry in California will be the legal profession.

Jobs-Killer California AB 32 Survives and Digs In

In 2006, the California Legislature passed and Gov. Arnold Schwarzenegger signed into law Assembly Bill 32, the Global Warming Solutions Act. This law mandates cuts of 25 percent in greenhouse gases emitted in the state by 2020, less than a decade away.[8] Imposition began in earnest in 2011.

Proposition 23 would have suspended AB 32 until state unemployment fell to 5.5 percent or below for a year. Given that state unemployment was 12.2 percent (seasonally adjusted) in February 2011, and given California's other economic problems, it is likely that 5.5 percent unemployment will not be reached in the next decade, even if a national economic recovery catches fire.

But Prop. 23 was wiped out by voters; it received just 39 percent of the vote, by far the lowest yea-vote percentage of any of the nine propositions on the ballot.[9] In the days leading to the election, polls showed that the proposition was trailing, but not that badly. We had hoped that with AB 32 digging in and destroying jobs, California voters might be inclined to stop the destruction. Prop. 23's clear defeat on November 2 probably ends such hopes. California will have to live with AB 32.

Meanwhile, AB 32 is gutting jobs. Earlier this year, Boeing transferred 800 jobs from Long Beach to Oklahoma City. Boeing did not give a reason, but critics blamed the move on the aerospace giant's fear of AB 32.[10] San Bernardino County Supervisor Brad Mitzelfelt warned that AB 32 basically will kill California's cement industry, currently the nation's largest, especially hitting the inland areas already suffering unemployment levels ranging from 15–30 percent.[11]

AB 32 gives the California Air Resources Board (CARB) vast new powers over the economy, including a new carbon trading scheme. On October 28, 2010, CARB announced its initial phase of the program. This shows what businesses in California will have to put up with now (in addition to all the other regulations and taxes):

SACRAMENTO - Today the California Air Resources Board announced the release of its proposed greenhouse gas cap-and-trade regulation....

A key part of CARB's AB 32 Scoping Plan, the cap-and-trade program provides an overall limit on the emissions from sources responsible for 85 percent of California's greenhouse gas emissions. This program allows covered entities the greatest flexibility for compliance, stimulates clean energy technologies, increases energy security and independence, protects public health and will drive clean, green jobs in California. It is designed to work in collaboration with other complementary policies that expand energy efficiency programs, reduce vehicle emissions, and encourage innovation.[12]

Other states and countries, of course, don't have to follow AB 32. Advocates of the ill-designed legislation maintain that it will create jobs in promising "green" industries. But the few jobs created would be overshadowed by up to 1.1 million jobs killed by its implementation, according to a study by the California Small Business Roundtable.[13]

As an additional note, the combined Los Angeles–Long Beach port system is by far the largest in the United States. San Francisco and San Diego also host major ports. Yet AB 32 regulations will force ships coming into these ports to slow down when crossing the Pacific in order to burn less fuel. Ports on the other side of the Panama Canal surely are licking their chops for 2014, when the new, enlarged canal will open. However, the U.S. Constitution gives the power to regulate foreign trade to the U.S. Congress, likely meaning lawsuits brought by shipping companies will thwart California's state level shipping regulations. Again we see more uncertainty—and another reason to avoid California entirely.

California Senate Bill 375

AB 32 is not the only massive new legislative assault on California businesses. In 2008, the Legislature passed and Gov. Schwarzenegger signed into law Senate Bill 375, the Redesigning Communities to Reduce Greenhouse Gases Act. Even the title is reminiscent of Soviet-era central planning. The governor's fact sheet explains:

The single-largest source of greenhouse gases in California is emissions from passenger vehicles, and in order to reduce those emissions, we must work to reduce Californians' vehicle-miles traveled (VMTs). That means helping people spend less time in their cars to get to work and to the grocery store. In order to reach California's greenhouse gas reductions goals set out in the Global Warming Solutions Act of 2006 (AB 32), we must rethink how we design our communities.

Senate Bill 375 by incoming Senator Pro Tem Darrell Steinberg would be the nation's first law to control greenhouse gas emissions by curbing sprawl. SB 375 provides emissions-reducing goals for which regions can plan, integrates disjointed planning activities, and provides incentives for local governments and developers to follow new conscientiously-planned growth patterns. SB 375 enhances the Air Resources Board's (ARB) ability to reach AB 32 goals.[14]

"Sprawl" is the central planners' epithet for nice suburban homes for the middle class, or California's style of living for the past century. SB 375—combined with AB 32—effectively gives CARB vast new authority to force Californians out of their homes into high-rises and out of their cars into mass transit. Moreover, by further increasing the cost of doing business in California, these regulations will drive more manufacturing and construction jobs from the state. Indeed, the continued exodus from California is being well-documented by Joseph Vranich, the "Business Relocation Coach," who notes that at least 204 companies had redirected capital out of California in 2010, compared to only 51 total in 2009.[15]

Unions Checkmated

On a positive note, voters in Arizona, North Carolina, North Dakota, and Utah voted to ban union card-check measures in their states. These "Save the Secret Ballot" initiatives provide a constitutional guarantee that workers cannot be bullied by union bosses to form a workplace union. These measures passed with more than 60 percent of the vote in Arizona and Utah and with more than 70 percent of the vote in South Carolina and South Dakota. This is good news all around since unions are trying to pass forced unionization bills at the federal level and in at least half of state legislatures.

Card-check, deceptively pushed at the federal level as the "Employee Free Choice Act," would eliminate secret ballots in union elections. Instead, a union would form automatically as long as more than 50 percent of workers sign a petition. Voters are not interested in eliminating secret ballots in elections, as they demonstrated clearly in Arizona, North Carolina, North Dakota, and Utah on Election Day. Card check bills essentially come down to the fact that their proponents believe unions need more power: To get more power they need more members and more money, and the way to do that is to change the rules.

Unions tend to have a negative impact on the economy, however. Excessive union influence appears to have been one of the pivotal factors that turned an economic downturn in 1929 into the Great Depression. According to a 2009 study by Lee Ohanian, an economics professor at UCLA and economist with the Federal Reserve Bank of Minneapolis, union influence caused companies to strike a deal that effectively, but artificially, increased real wages for manufacturer workers in the midst of a recession.[16] The result is precisely what economics would predict: employers could no longer afford to pay workers for the same number of hours they had been working prior to the wage increases.

In what has been a very positive trend for the U.S. economy, the total percentage of the U.S. workforce with union membership has been declining steadily and steeply for approximately 30 years. However, this trend reversed in 2008 (see Figure 6). Based on the policies and priorities of the Obama administration, this reversal may persist for many years.

In our view, the explanation for the decline in union strength for the previous 30 years in all areas except government is simple enough: Unions place firms at a competitive disadvantage, and

they do little to benefit workers directly. As the forces of globalization make business more and more competitive, American firms cannot survive if they are hobbled by inefficient labor arrangements demanded by union leaders. Furthermore, many union members vehemently disagree with the way union leaders use their union dues for political purposes.[17]

As long as a labor market is competitive, workers are generally paid equal to their marginal product of labor. This is not because of an employer's sense of benevolence or fair play; instead it is because of the competition between firms. If a particular worker annually adds $50,000 to a firm's bottom line while he earns only $45,000, a rival firm can afford to try to lure him away by offering to pay him up to $5,000 more than his current employer is paying. To avoid losing effective employees, it is in employers' best interest to pay workers according to the value they create.

Unions certainly do not change these fundamental facts for the better. Although they might serve to reduce transactions costs when negotiating arrangements between employers and huge pools of workers, unions typically achieve deals (through threats of strikes or worse) that force a firm to pay more total compensation (in the form of wages, health insurance, and other benefits) than is justified by an employee's marginal product. Unions also tend to negotiate counterproductive or excessive work rules, vacation time, sick leave, health benefits, pension benefits, and so forth; they tend to be very political and work to enforce their ends via political means.

All of these excessive costs above a worker's actual output erode the firm's profits and leave it vulnerable to other firms. A nonunion firm, presumably operating at a point where the real wage is equal to the marginal product of labor, can easily undercut unionized firms and steal their customers, their business, and their profits. In a competitive industry, unionization has a devastating effect on a firm's profits. In the long run, unionized firms are forced to shut down because nonunion firms seize the business by selling a similar good at a lower cost. When a firm shuts down, the union workers are out of luck and out of work. This outcome does not benefit the workers in the unionized firm.

The recent experience of General Motors, Chrysler, and Ford should remove any doubts

FIGURE 6 | **Annual Union Membership as a Percentage of Total U.S. Workforce, 1948-2008**

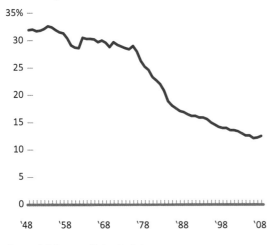

Source: U.S. Bureau of Labor Statistics

concerning the devastating impact unions can have on the future viability of a company or industry. Unions do not just have a negative impact on private industry, though. The unions dominate state government in California, more so now than in 1990, and that power is growing every day. The power they hold is frightening. California's pension systems are far worse today than they were in 1990. Pensions for state teachers and other state employees, as well as those for city, county, and local district employees, are drastically underfunded. Public sector unions are literally bankrupting the state to an extent we have never before witnessed. That is precisely why unions were fading away as global competition intensified.

It is for these reasons that unions find their only refuge in government jobs. Competition and quality products are not union attributes. Experience with the Department of Motor Vehicles, public schools, or public prisons gives credence to this assessment.

Health Care Freedom

In Arizona, Colorado, and Oklahoma, the electorate voted on a key feature of the new ObamaCare law. These initiatives preserve the right of citizens in these states not to purchase health insurance. Arizona and Oklahoma voters easily approved these "health care choice" measures, but Coloradans voted no. These were voter referendums on ObamaCare, and the results show that voters are not wild about what Barack Obama calls his most historic achievement. Missouri voters passed ALEC's Freedom of Choice in Health Care Act in 2010, with 71 percent of the vote.

All of the uncertainty regarding the specifics of implementation of President Obama's health care reform notwithstanding, the economics is straightforward. From the standpoint of Econ 101, a market keeps check on prices and costs through a dynamic interchange between suppliers of products and demanders of products. When a person walks into a store he has a vast array of wants and needs and a budget. Whenever a product is too pricey, the consumer either buys less or abstains from buying any of it at all. On seeing sales fall, suppliers either lower their prices or withdraw some supply from the marketplace.

This is a no brainer. Consumers of any product keep suppliers in check and control prices. Health care services are no different than any

other product. But when health care expenditures are covered by private insurance or public funds, individual consumers care less about price and, thus, exercise less control over unwarranted price increases. Consumers also tend to consume larger quantities of the higher priced products than they would were they required to pay for those products out of their own pockets. It really is as simple as that. As former U.S. Sen. Phil Gramm of Texas notes, if he had to pay only five cents for each dollar of groceries he bought, he would eat really well—and so would his dog. Consumers who do not have to pay the full price for each additional unit they buy will consume more than they need. That is Econ 101.

The huge increase in health care costs over the past half century has been greatly exacerbated by the sharp decline in the percentage of health care costs paid for by individuals out of their own pockets and the ever-increasing role played by the government and private insurance.

In Figure 7 we have plotted the shares of health care expenditures paid for by individuals, government, and private insurance.

ObamaCare displays a fundamental lack of understanding of basic economics, as its mandates for more government and more insurance starkly demonstrate. Voters in Arizona, Missouri, and Oklahoma were wise to strike down part of health care reform, and we hope more states follow in their footsteps.

FIGURE 7 | Share of Health Care Spending Paid by Individuals, Government, and Private Insurance, 1960-2008

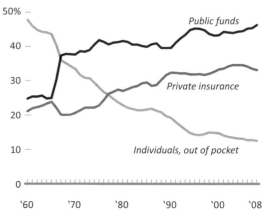

Source: Centers for Medicare and Medicaid Services

Other State Ballot Highlights
Tax Measures

Georgians passed Referendum A, which exempts business inventories from state property taxes.

Indiana passed Question 1, which will cap property taxes at 1 percent, rental property in residential areas at 2 percent, and taxes for business at 3 percent. Though these are not as stringent as limits in other states, advocates believe the caps will protect residents of Indiana from wild increases in property tax payments.[18]

Louisiana passed one of the most fiscally consequential measures of any state. Its Amendment 6 requires a two-thirds majority vote in the Legislature to authorize any benefit for state employees if the benefit is a cost to the taxpayers. In Louisiana, as in so many states, public pensions and health plans are bankrupting taxpayers. The unfunded liabilities of states and cities for government employee benefits are estimated at between $2 and $3 trillion.[19] Let us hope this is the start of a trend to reign in bloated state pensions.

Missouri voters overwhelmingly approved a measure to prohibit cities from enacting an income/wage tax and phases out the wage tax in St. Louis and Kansas City. The language reads as follows:

> Proposition A repeals the authority for cities to levy an earnings tax, require voter approval for the continuation of earnings taxes in Kansas City and St. Louis at the next municipal election and every five years thereafter, require any earnings tax not approved by voters to be phased out over 10 years, and prohibit all cities in Missouri from imposing a new earnings tax.[20]

This initiative was sponsored by Rex Sinquefield, president of the St. Louis–based Show-Me Institute. The data show persuasively that cities with income and wage taxes have lower job growth and capital investment.

The results in Massachusetts were more mixed. The bad news there: Massachusetts voters rejected a plan to halve the state sales tax. The good news: they also rejected a bill passed by the legislature to impose a new tax on alcohol.[21]

Other Measures

One of the most disappointing Election Day outcomes was Florida voters' rejection of Amendment 8, which would have repealed a constitutional class size mandate in public schools. Had it passed, the amendment would have allowed flexibility for districts in meeting class size reduction requirements. The measure that mandates minimum class sizes in Florida schools is expected to cost the state $40 billion over the next 20 years. This triumph for the teachers' unions puts Florida in a deep fiscal hole going forward.[22]

Also in Florida, 52 percent voted to overturn the state's wasteful public campaign finance option, but 60 percent was needed for passage.[23] Floridians also approved Referendum 1 for a balanced budget amendment to the U.S. Constitution.[24]

Here is one of our favorites: Illinois made it easier for voters to recall the governor. Call it the Blagojevich law.[25]

Montana voters passed Initiative 105 to prohibit state or local governments from imposing any new taxes on transactions that sell or transfer real property.[26] A very bad initiative passed as well, though; Initiative 164 caps annual interest rates of payday loans at 36 percent.[27] These restrictive rate caps on short loans could put payday lenders out of business, which would eliminate a financial option for struggling residents living paycheck to paycheck.

Oklahoma wisely defeated Question 744, which would have required the legislature to fund public education to at least the per pupil average of neighboring states.[28] While this was a dream of the teachers' unions, higher per pupil spending has not necessarily led to improved education.

Conclusion

It was a wild year politically. Yet while the federal elections stole the show, a number of interesting battles were fought through state ballot initiatives. Kudos to those states that moved toward pro-growth policies or fought off policies that discourage production. Kudos to Washington state in particular for its bold stand against the institution of a state income tax on the "rich."

ENDNOTES

1 Gunn, Amber. "Washington Voters Reject State Income Tax Proposal." *Budget and Tax News.* January 2011.

2 *Facts and Figures on Government Finance.* 38th edition. Tax Foundation. 2004.

3 "Washingtonians Who Get It." *The Wall Street Journal.* November 7, 2010.

4 Bailey, Ronald. "Green Machine Myth." *Monterey County Weekly.* February 17, 2011.

5 For background on California's Proposition 13, please see: Laffer, Arthur, Moore, Stephen and Williams, Jonathan. *Rich States, Poor States.* American Legislative Exchange Council. 2009.

6 Associated Press. "Budget Passed but Inherent Deficit Problems Remain." *Appeal-Democrat.* October 8, 2010.

7 Lomax, Simon. "California Vote May 'Stifle' Environmental Laws." *Bloomberg Businessweek.* November 3, 2010.

8 Lifsher, Marc. "Climate shifts on Global-Warming Law." *Los Angeles Times.* October 24, 2006.

9 Bowen, Debra. "Statement of Vote, November 2, 2010, General Election." California Secretary of State. Revised January 6, 2011.

10 Plazak, Doug. "AB32 Already Costing the State Jobs." *Orange County Register.* September 27, 2010.

11 Lindstorm, Natasha. "Mitzelfelt Spills Why He Thinks AB32 Is 'Insanity.'" *Daily Press.* February 8, 2010.

12 California Environmental Protection Agency, Air Resources Board. "Proposed California Greenhouse Gas Emissions Trading Program Now Available." News release. October 28, 2010.

13 Varshney and Associates on behalf of Betty Jo Toccoli and California Small Business Roundtable. "Cost of AB 32 on California Small Business—Summary Report of Findings." June 2009.

14 Office of the Governor, Arnold Schwarzenegger. "Fact Sheet: Senate Bill 375: Redesigning Communities to Reduce Greenhouse Gases." October 1, 2008.

15 Vranich, Joe. "Part 1: Record in 2010 for California Companies Departing or Diverting Capital: Four Times Last Year's Level." *The Business Relocation Coach.* January 26, 2011.

16 Ohanian, Lee. "What—or Who—Started the Great Depression?" *Journal of Economic Theory.* July 29, 2009.

17 "New Nationwide Poll Shows Union Members Support Right to Work." National Right to Work Committee. October 2010.

18. Merrick, Amy. "Indiana Embraces Tax Caps Despite Hit to City Services." *The Wall Street Journal.* January 30, 2010.

19. Beaird, Wanda. "Amendment 6: Voters to Consider Legislative Votes for Retirement Benefit Changes." *Leesville Daily Leader.* October 26, 2010.

20. "2010 Ballot Measures." Missouri Secretary of State. 2010.

21. Nickisch, Curt. "Mass. Voters Keep Sales Tax, But Repeal It on Alcohol." WBUR.com. November 3, 2010.

22. Goodman, Josh. "Amendment 8 Class-Size Vote Puts Florida Lawmakers in a Bind." Stateline.org. November 5, 2010.

23. Klas, Mary Ellen. "Rick Scott's Challenge of Florida Public Campaign finance Law Tossed out of Court." *St. Petersburg Times.* July 15, 2010.

24. "Referendum for 2010 General Election." Florida Division of Elections. 2010.

25. Long, Ray. "Illinois Voters to Decide Recall Power." *Chicago Tribune.* October 31, 2010.

26. "Constitutional Initiative No. 105 (CI-105)." Montana Secretary of State. 2010.

27. "Initiative No. 164 (I-164)." Montana Secretary of State. 2010.

28. Rolland, Megan. "Oklahoma Election: Heated Battle for State Question 744 Ends in Defeat." *NewsOK.* November 2, 2010.

Prosperity 101:
Lessons for State Economic Growth

Prosperity 101:
Lessons for State Economic Growth

I n the last several years we have witnessed some of the most misguided economic policies in decades, both at the federal and state levels. In many cases, sound economic policies that create jobs and prosperity have been tossed aside for gimmicks and old mistakes.

These policy errors have been so plentiful and so fundamentally backwards we are compelled to go back to the basics and ask some elemental questions. What causes prosperity? How does a nation or a state create jobs? Which policies have worked throughout history to generate economic growth in a state or country, and which have not? This is written for lawmakers and other decision makers in state capitals and in Washington, D.C. We call this chapter Prosperity 101 because it offers a simple-to-understand roadmap for regaining prosperity given the economic havoc that has reigned now for several years.

The Tragedy of "Obamanomics"

The verdict is in: The $3 trillion experiment in government as the solution to our economic problems has been a resounding failure.[1] When the economy collapsed in 2008, almost every step the Bush administration, the Obama administration, and the Federal Reserve Board took made the economy worse, not better.

The damage from the stock market contraction and bank failures could have been contained and short lived, if not for a series of disastrous policy strategies in Washington. The politicians could not keep from intervening over and over again. And that combination of policy malfeasance, ignorance, and arrogance has put America into a $14 trillion debt spiral for which our children, our grandchildren, and our great-grandchildren will have to pay.[2]

In this stage of the economic recovery, June 2011, the economy is growing, but much more slowly than we would expect. During the early stages of the Reagan expansion in 1983–84, the economy grew by as much as 8 percent—more than three times faster than the pace of growth we have seen over the past year. The unemployment rate set a post-World War II record, staying above 9 percent for 21 straight months.[3] The stimulus was supposed to create 3 million jobs; instead it has corresponded with the loss of 2 million.[4]

Some liberals say President Obama did not spend enough, but this is sheer fantasy. Rarely have we witnessed such a deluge of new spending in the nation's history. The Santa Claus spending agenda was signed into law within 40 days of the new presidency: What a victory for liberalism. American families tightened their belts, cut expenses, saved more, worked harder, and paid off debts, while in Washington it was like Christmas, Easter, and the 4th of July all wrapped into one gigantic spending party. Agencies were so flush with stimulus cash, they could not spend fast enough. Money was allocated for myriad projects ranging from golf carts for federal workers to a mouse eradication project in Nancy Pelosi's congressional district.[5] While Americans suffered through a horrid recession, the government celebrated as if happy days were here again.

The height of the folly came with the Obama administration's Cash for Clunkers program, which paid Americans $3,500–$4,500 to trade in old cars if they were buying new cars with better gas mileage.[6] This program of free money for clunkers was wildly popular: Americans rushed to new car showrooms to get their checks, some for ten times the trade-in value of their cars. They were winning the lottery.

Of course, taking good cars off the road and destroying them so people will buy new cars is as economically illiterate as using rocks and sledgehammers to break the windows of buildings so people will be put to work and paid handsomely for the repairs. The fallacy of logic here was exposed in the unforgettable book, *Economics in One Lesson*, by Henry Hazlett. Money spent on window repairs and unnecessary new cars is money that cannot be spent on home renovations or new washing machines. In other words, while the destruction of valuable goods may benefit the industry called upon for repair or replacement in the short term, it imposes a long term cost on society and removes value from the economy that may otherwise have created even more wealth. As our friend John Stossel explains it, "leave it to politicians to think we can prosper by obliterating wealth."[7]

Despite Cash for Clunkers, America continued to lose jobs—though, yes, auto jobs increased temporarily as we paid people to buy new cars. In addition to increased spending, the Obama administration worked to continue the nationalization of industry that began with banks, mortgage companies, insurance firms, and Wall Street investment houses. Next on the docket was a multibillion-dollar takeover of the auto industry. Chrysler and General Motors were to be rescued by Washington—but really the entity being saved was the United Auto Workers union.

We witnessed a ham-handed, and possibly unconstitutional bankruptcy designed by the unions and the White House. This was not a normal bankruptcy. Instead, the federal government essentially stole $3–$5 billion rightfully owned by the GM and Chrysler creditors—the owners of the car companies' secured debt—and secured the money for the unions. This conflicted with centuries of corporate contract law that says creditors are first in line to claim a company's assets. Creditors should be paid before other stakeholders, like shareholders and workers. In this case, the Obama administration ripped up the creditors' contracts and strong-armed the bondholders into taking pennies on the dollars they were owed. At the time of the crisis, Richard Mourdock, the Treasurer of the State of Indiana, testified before the Congressional Oversight Panel. In his testimony, Mourdock asked the panel, "If the term "secured creditor" no longer has meaning, what other terms of art in the world of finance

no longer have meaning?" He warned the panel, "Change the rules and the players will change. If foreign investors in U.S. Treasury debt sense that "good faith and credit of the United States government" can be swept away with an arbitrary act to deal with a momentary crisis, we will have a problem far, far greater than Chrysler in scope and impact."[8] We could not agree more with Mr. Mourdock. Unfortunately with their shoulders to the wheel, this administration brushed off the warning and continued to drive us to the cliff.

President Obama even publicly castigated the hedge funds that owned many of these bonds for their lack of cooperation and selfishness. Rich hedge fund managers were not being looted, though; pension funds and those with IRAs and 401(k) plans invested in the auto companies saw their savings pillaged for the sake of union bosses. The long term effects of the government's voiding contract law for political expedience may be devastating.

Meanwhile, the Federal Reserve Board, under the management of Chairman Ben Bernanke, delegated to itself exceptional powers to save the United States from another Great Depression. The Fed played an instrumental role in orchestrating the bank bailouts. It helped manipulate who would run which companies—which CEOs were in, which were out. It helped mastermind the merger of Merrill Lynch and Bank of America—threatening to crush Bank of America if it refused to take on the struggling company. The constitutionality of these actions is suspect, but Mr. Bernanke was acting as the savior of the global financial system. This apparently means rules, like those in the Constitution, could be bent or expended.

Recently, the Fed adopted a policy called Quantitative Easing (QE-2), which is a fancy way of saying it will print $600 billion to purchase federal debt.[9] This is supposed to create jobs, but it is more likely to create higher prices. The Fed can print money, but it cannot print jobs.

The total costs of bailouts, stimulus plans, Fed-orchestrated buyouts, and so forth have already totaled in the trillions.[10] That is a mighty high price tag. Was it worth it?

Free Lunch Economics

The trillions already spent is a huge sum of money and eventually the bill will come due—bills always do. The tragedy in all this spending is that it was unnecessary: For all that was devoted to picking winners and losers in the economy, Congress simply could have suspended the federal income tax for 18 months. This would have been a far less expensive and much more effective tonic for the economy. Imagine if all businesses and workers had been notified they could keep everything they earned—there would be no income tax withholding, no business profits taxes, no taxes on savings and investment; the economy would have recovered at breakneck speed and jobs lost would have been a fraction of what they have been.

The Keynesian premise under which the Obama administration has been operating—that government spending on make-work projects puts the economy back on its feet—is highly disputable. The theory is that government should spend money and create demand for goods and services to keep the economy afloat as consumers are reluctant to spend during a recession. This is exemplified when we hear the happy talk of the Keynesian multiplier, the claim that $1 in additional government spending translates to $2 or $3 additional economic output because the money circulates many times throughout the economy.

There is a big hole in this theory and an even bigger problem with its real life track record. The theory is leaky because it ignores a basic premise of economics: As Milton Friedman famously taught many years ago, "There's no such thing as a free lunch." There is no fairy who magically endows the economy with dollars for the government to spend. It is not that simple.

The money the government spends originates somewhere. The government obtains dollars to spend in three ways: by borrowing, taxing, and printing. Each of these options carries negative consequences that outweigh any positive effects of the government's spending.

If it borrows the money, someone has to buy the bonds the government issues so the money can be spent. Every borrowed dollar the government spends is first taken out of the economy through the purchase of these bonds. (While foreigners do purchase about half of these bonds, the costs associated with foreign debt ownership may even be worse.) At best, the net effect of government borrowing on stimulating the economy is zero.

If the government raises taxes to obtain the money to spend, the cost to the economy is higher. In this scenario, dollars are taken from productive workers who earned the money with their labor and given to people and government agencies that did not earn the money. The net effect of this redistribution scheme is negative because there is a 20–30 cents per dollar cost associated with collecting taxes. While the recipient of the tax dollar may spend that money at McDonalds or Walmart to create a multiplier effect, it costs the economy $1.20 or more to get that dollar circulating after the taxman plays his part.

Finally, if the government obtains money by printing more dollars, the value of all other dollars is reduced. In other words, if the government magically doubled the supply of money—all else being equal—the value of every dollar would be half what it was. If printing money were the ticket to wealth creation, Argentina, Bolivia, and Mexico would be rolling in prosperity.

The costs associated with obtaining money for government spending represent a major flaw in the Keynesian theory. An examination of the real-life impact "stimulus plans" have had in the past demonstrates that the theory has not held true in practice either. First, let us look at the New Deal. This was the largest peacetime experiment—until now—of government spending as stimulus. President Franklin Delano Roosevelt was elected in 1932 in the midst of the Great Depression, and upon taking office he launched what became known as an alphabet soup of government programs to combat unemployment. Government expenditures rose over 83 percent; funds were used to pay for new jobs programs, agriculture programs, welfare, Social Security, and similar programs.[11] Under the New Deal, the federal government burned crops in the field to reduce the supply of food in an effort to keep food prices high.[12] The government believed doing so would help raise farmers' incomes. Meanwhile, as the government was destroying crops, cities were filled with tens of thousands of Americans who were going to bed hungry each night due to a lack of income and food shortages.

Tragically, none of the New Deal programs worked. The more the government spent and borrowed (the federal debt rose by a then unthinkable level for peacetime), the more the economy contracted. Even FDR's own Treasury Secretary

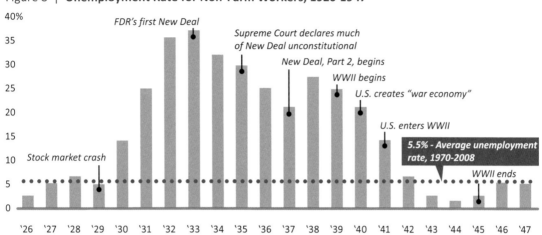

Figure 8 | **Unemployment Rate for Non-Farm Workers, 1926-1947**

Source: The Heritage Foundation

declared the spending barrage a failure at getting Americans back to work.[13] School books celebrate the New Deal as a success, but the actual data show it as an abject failure and responsible for prolonging depression economic conditions.[14] Figure 8 shows that during the Great Depression, President Roosevelt's New Deal programs failed to bring the unemployment lower than 20 percent. The jobless rate actually rose after the second phase.[15]

There is also a more contemporary example showing the failures of Keynesian demand-side economics. Japan tried several fiscal stimulus plans in the 1990s and early 2000s in an effort to end the nearly two-decade depression that started in 1991. The whole country was paved in concrete through public works programs; even parts of the ocean were paved over when they were finished on the land. What was the result of this borrow and spend stimulus? Japan's budget transformed from a 2 percent surplus of GDP in 1990 to an 8 percent deficit of GDP in 2002.[16] After years of government pump priming, a substantial amount of the country's financial wealth had disappeared. This is hardly a model we should emulate.

All Debt Is Not Created Equal

President Ronald Reagan's administration incurred $2 trillion of debt in the 1980s, but that debt accomplished two missions of great long-term consequence. First, it helped finance the Cold War military buildup that helped free the

world from communist tyranny. Second, it financed tax rate reductions that helped rebuild the U.S. economy after the stagflation the economy suffered under President Jimmy Carter in the 1970s. Although the debt rose by $2 trillion under President Reagan, national wealth increased by at least $6 trillion.[17] Despite the evidence that tax rate reductions have worked to spur economic growth, the Obamanomics agenda was centered on Keynesian economic theories that have yet to work in practice and did not include any pro-growth tax cuts.[18]

What Does Lead to Growth?

The policy ideas that lead to prosperity are those that are consistent with promoting economic freedom. This is true for countries and states. Countries with more economic freedom have strong property rights, low taxes, light regulation, free trade, sound money, right of contract, private operation of business, and other such measures that limit undue government interference in the market. In general, interference with the free market inhibits growth.[19]

Figure 9 on page 38 succinctly demonstrates how economic freedom leads to growth. It shows that the countries that adhere most closely to the principles of economic freedom, as measured by the Cato Institute, have had the most success in raising the living standards of their citizens. We have consistently found the same principle to be true for states. Americans, because we live in a

Figure 9 | Economic Freedom: Free Countries are Wealthier and Healthier

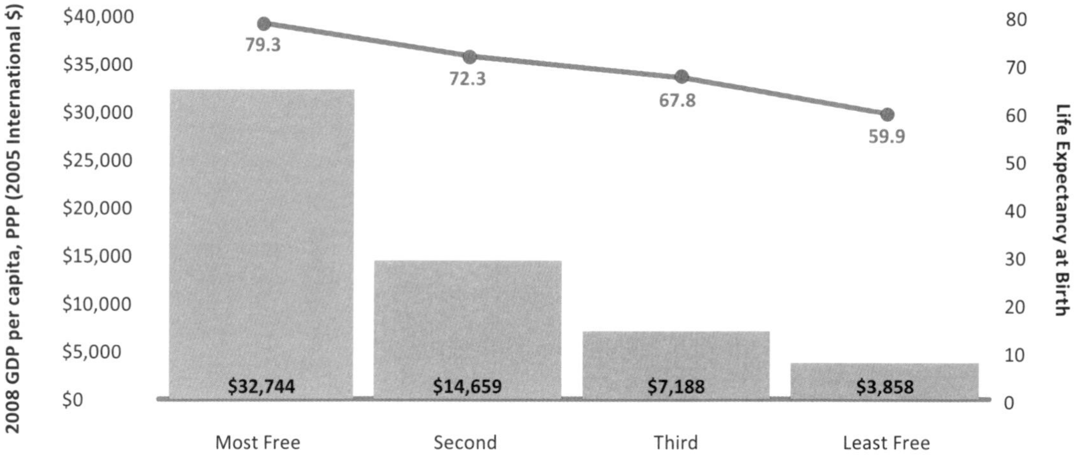

Source: Cato Institute and Fraser Institute

country that is mostly free (though moving in the wrong direction in some regards), have a living standard that is roughly ten times higher than that of those living in countries that repress the market and do not respect individual rights.

Figure 9 is instructive for another reason. Some critics say free markets, although they create growth, cause other problems, such as social inequities, pollution, and other injustices. We looked at another measure of well-being: health, as measured by life expectancy. We found that economic freedom is also highly correlated with a higher life expectancy. Free countries like the United States have average life expectancies nearly twenty years longer than socialized countries that do not respect private property. This means economically free countries are not just wealthier, they are also healthier. Other studies have found that economic freedom is highly correlated with reductions in pollution levels as well.[20] The evidence is clear that freedom, low taxes, and prosperity are the best medicines for whatever ails a state. This section will examine some of these important principles for economic freedom and, consequently,

Figure 10 | Share the Wealth?
Top Marginal Income Tax Rates and Income Tax Share for the Top Percent of Earners, 1970-2008

Source: U.S. Internal Revenue Service

growth: keeping taxes low, guarding against inflation, and keeping budgets in check.

Principle 1: Keep Tax Rates Low

President Reagan understood the importance of keeping tax rates low better than any president in recent history. The tax cuts made under the Reagan administration were inspired in large part by his experience as an actor. As he explained, actors in his day would make only three movies in a year. If they made a fourth, their tax rate would go up to such an extent that it would be unprofitable. President Reagan recognized that the same logic applied in other sectors of the economy, and in August 1981, he signed into law the largest tax-rate cut in history. When President Reagan took office in 1981, the top marginal tax rate on individuals was 70 percent. By the time Ronald Reagan left office in 1989, the top marginal rate was reduced to 28 percent.[21] Amazing but true.

With Paul Volcker at the helm of the Federal Reserve, President Reagan also reined in inflation and moved swiftly to lift many burdensome regulations. His administration marked the beginning of the greatest period of prosperity in the history of the world. America's net worth climbed in real terms from $25 trillion in 1980 to nearly $57 trillion in 2010.[22] Between 1981 and today, more wealth was created than in the previous 200 years.[23]

The policy works for Republicans as well as Democrats. President John F. Kennedy's supply-side tax cuts in 1961 serve as a shining example of good policy overcoming partisanship. President Kennedy knew high tax rates were restricting growth so much that the federal government could actually increase revenues by cutting taxes. It is increasingly clear that no matter which party is in power—as long as our national security needs keep rising—what President Kennedy said in a 1963 speech to the Economic Club of New York remains true: "An economy constrained by high tax rates will never produce enough revenue to balance the budget, just as it will never create enough jobs."[24] Nor will an economy restricted by high tax rates produce profits sufficient to counteract government spending.

Figure 10 on page 38 confirms that President Kennedy was right. When tax rates have fallen at the federal level, the share of taxes paid by the wealthy has increased. In 1980, when the top tax rate was 70 percent, the wealthiest 1 percent of Americans paid a little less than 20 percent of all federal income taxes. By 2007, when the top tax rate was 35 percent—half what it was in 1980—the share of taxes paid by the wealthy rose to 41 percent.

Lowering tax rates increases the incentive to work and invest. As marginal tax rates decrease, the incentive to invest in the United States also increases. Lower personal and corporate tax rates attract investment by making it possible for businesses to be more profitable. Thus, lower rates encourage new firms to enter the market and may entice established firms to relocate.

The U.S. tax system is especially uncompetitive in this area: the country's corporate tax rate now ranks second highest in the world when state business tax rates are included.[25] Figure 11 shows that the trend is unfavorable to the United States. In the 1980s and early 1990s, the U.S. corporate tax rate was below the average rate of our competitor countries. Now, the U.S. rate is significantly higher than the average of developed countries— nearly 15 percentage points higher. Even Sweden has a lower corporate tax rate than the combined state/federal rate in most of the 50 states. Almost everyone, including the Obama administration's own tax reform commission, believes this puts the United States at a competitive disadvantage and costs America jobs.[26] States with high corporate tax rates—including California, New

Figure 11 | **U.S. Corporate Tax Rate Versus Average in OECD Countries, 1990-2010**

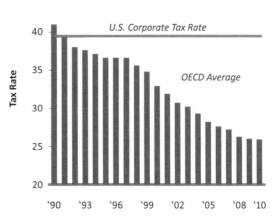

Source: Organization for Economic Cooperation and Development

TABLE 6 | **Flat Tax Countries and Their Rates**

Country	Rate
Albania	10%
Bulgaria	10
Czech Republic	15
Estonia	21
Georgia	12
Guernsey	20
Hong Kong	15
Iceland	35.7
Iraq	15
Jamaica	25
Jersey	20
Kazakhstan	10
Kyrgyzstan	10
Latvia	25
Lithuania	27
Macedonia	10
Mauritius	15
Montenegro	15
Mongolia	10
Pridnestrovie	10
Romania	16
Russia	13
Slovakia	19
Ukraine	15

Source: Center for Freedom and Prosperity

York, Iowa, and Illinois—have the highest combined federal and state corporate tax rate among all members of the Organization for Economic Cooperation and Development (OECD). This is a sure way to export jobs out of these states and out of the United States entirely. Reducing state and federal business taxes should be a high priority for state lawmakers.

Keep the United States Competitive

In addition to addressing corporate tax rates to make the country more competitive, the United States should consider a more holistic change in tax policy. In the past couple of decades, the rest of the world began to understand the virtues of supply-side economics while the U.S. government understanding appears to have regressed. Many countries formerly under socialism now embrace tax systems far more pro-growth than the U.S. tax system.

It is time for a flat tax in America. Table 6 shows that many countries around the world have adopted flat taxes. A flat tax of 15-20 percent would attract investment and jobs to the United States like a giant high-voltage magnet. It would also simplify the tax code and reduce special interest loopholes high-powered lobbyists have carved out for their clients.

Lowering tax rates is also an important way to attract capital. As Figure 12 shows, the United States transitioned from a country exporting capital in the 1970s to one importing capital after tax

Figure 12 | **Tax Cuts Attract Capital**

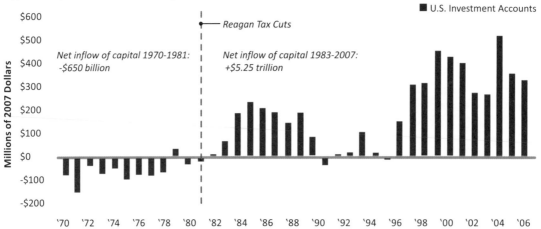

Source: Bureau of Economic Analysis

rates fell in the 1980s. In the 25 years following the Reagan tax cuts, net imports of capital in the United States from the rest of the world totaled $5.25 trillion.[27] States can expect the same effect: When a state's tax rates fall, capital owners and business leaders from other states and countries will want to invest in that state.

The Laffer Curve

The Laffer Curve shows why lower tax rates result in greater tax payments by the rich. Arthur Laffer's legendary napkin sketch started a pro-growth revolution. Tax rates that are too high

prohibit growth and decrease incentives to work, save, and invest. Decreasing marginal tax rates increases these incentives and, when this results in economic growth, can also increase revenue.

As the Laffer Curve to the left demonstrates, there are two tax rates that will produce the same level of revenue. When tax rates are at 100 percent, there is no incentive to work, so no revenues are produced for the government. The curve shows that tax rates can be so high they cause the government to lose revenue. This holds true at both federal and state levels. The ideal tax rate is that which produces the most growth, though this is often well below the revenue maximizing rate. For states, the growth maximizing income tax rate is ... zero.

The Laffer Curve does not work only on a blackboard. It has also held true in practice. Figure 14 shows that decreases in tax rates have resulted in increased revenues to the federal government; the same results can hold true at the state level. In the 1980s, the government's total tax revenues doubled even as tax rates fell by more than half.

The often maligned Bush tax cuts created jobs at a near record pace. Reduced tax rates for employers and investors created incentives for job creation, and businesses responded. Increasing tax rates slows the pace job creation.

After the Bush tax cuts, employment soared. Unfortunately, many of these gains have been

Figure 13 | **The Laffer Curve**

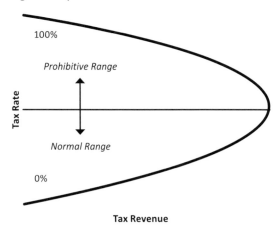

Source: Laffer Associates

Figure 14 | **Real Federal Revenues and the Top Marginal Income Tax Rate**

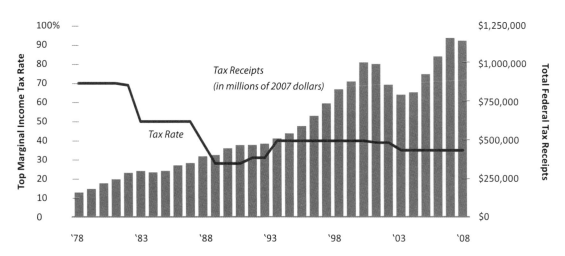

Source: U.S. Office of Management and Budget, Budget of the United States Government, *Fiscal Year 2008*

wiped away by the financial crisis. Another supply-side stimulus is needed to get employment back on track today.

President Obama and the Congress extended the Bush tax cuts for another two years in December 2010, but the cuts are scheduled to expire after 2012. This would be catastrophic for the U.S. economy. Taxes as a share of GDP will reach an all-time high if tax rates return to what they were prior to the Bush cuts. Since federal taxpayers are also state taxpayers, the more money Washington takes from taxpayers, the harder it will be for states to balance their budgets.

Do Tax Cuts Hurt the Middle Class?

It is an often repeated myth in the U.S. economy that tax cuts benefit only the wealthy while causing the middle class and poor to fall further behind. In reality, the middle class has made significant economic gains over the past three decades, that is, since tax rates started falling. The hallmark of the U.S. economy over the past several decades has been upward economic mobility. Many people have moved to higher income classes over time, though some have fallen. This upward mobility occurs because the United States is a country based on opportunity; it needs to remain a nation where people can rise and fall based on their work, entrepreneurship, and talent.

Figure 15 tells the real story about America's middle class. The middle class, defined as the middle quintile of American families, earns more money today than in the 1950s, 70s, or 90s. Those considered middle class has changed from those making between $33,408 and $44,800 in 1967 to those making between $45,021 and $68,304 in 2005 (in inflation adjusted terms). Middle class incomes are not shrinking, but growing. However, families suffered income losses during the 2008–2009 recession that may not be recovered for years.

Principle 2: Guard Against Inflation

Inflation kills jobs. This was evident in the 1970s when the economy was in the tank and the inflation rate skyrocketed. At one point the inflation rate hit 14 percent under President Carter.[28] High inflation rates hurt the states and caused increased costs for the things states buy. State deficits rose as inflation rose. States should not be advocates of high inflation; they should support stable currency policies.

Education and health care are two industries largely provided by government, particularly state government. These two industries have had nearly the highest rates of inflation over the past decade. The third-party payer system in both industries is one of the biggest reasons for this. A third party often pays for health care—whether insurers or government—and for education—through government or scholarship programs. This protects the patient or student from the full cost of health care and education. Reducing subsidies for health care and education would help prevent the inflation these industries continue to suffer, and it would be best if the financial resources were given directly to the payer—the patient or student—instead of to the provider of care or education. This could be done through vouchers or other means. Health care and education are two of the largest items in state budgets; governors and legislators will have difficulty balancing their budgets without reforming these programs.

Figure 16 shows the inflation rates in education, health care, and several other items. It also documents the benefits of trade—whether among states or between countries: Prices for many consumer items have fallen over the past decade, especially for those items directly affected by trade. Imports lower prices to consumers. Lower prices enable consumers to get more for their paychecks, thereby increasing their real standard of living.

Figure 15 | Upper and Lower Income Limits for Middle Class Families (in 2005 dollars)

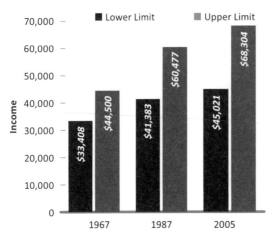

Source: U.S. Internal Revenue Service

Principle 3: Balance the Budget

It is clear that inflation puts extra pressure on states' finances. As mentioned previously, policies to address the inflation related to large state expenditures like health care and education will be necessary to enable states to keep their budgets in check. Government budgets should be lean and balanced; this is important for encouraging economic growth and should be a primary focus of state governments.

The exploding federal budget presents a lesson to states of what not to do to help their economies grow. The budget was fairly constrained in the 1990s under President Bill Clinton and a Republican controlled Congress. The budget was balanced as a result of expenditure controls and strong economic growth that generated massive revenues for the federal government and the states. But over the past decade both parties went on an unprecedented spending binge. President Obama inherited a $500 billion deficit, and through his spending policies, he allowed that budget deficit to reach $1.3 trillion. This is not a pretty picture.

Politicians in Washington talk about an infrastructure deficit or a shortage of dollars for other public programs, but the federal budget has been growing rapidly for the past decade. Most programs have grown at three or four times the rate of inflation. It is time for tight lids on federal spending and a return to 2007 levels of outlays to enable the United States to begin to bring the federal deficit under control.

Principle 4: More Spending is Not the Answer

One of the most enduring public policy lessons every state lawmaker must take to heart is that government spending and debt do not create jobs. American politicians—in Washington and in the states—should pay careful attention to the policy lessons from the financial turmoil in Greece, Ireland, Portugal, and other big spending European nations. The EU has had to intervene with a $1 trillion bailout that grows each month.[29] If there is any good that can come from this Greek calamity, which could spread to other nations in Europe, it is that we are witnessing firsthand the corrosive consequences of the economic theories of John Maynard Keynes.[30]

The story is fairly simple: Two years ago, as the worldwide economic recession deepened, political leaders in the United States and Europe flocked to the ideas of Mr. Keynes and his disciples, who advised mountainous government-spending plans financed by debt to revive flagging economies. The consensus opinion from economists at the International Monetary Fund (IMF), the World Bank, Harvard's faculty, and the Obama administration was to ramp up government spending to accelerate aggregate demand.[31] They believed Keynesian government spending injections would rescue the world economy from another Great Depression.

Princeton economist Alan S. Blinder wrote that according to the theory behind this policy prescription, public sector spending causes a "multiplier effect; that is, output increases by a multiple of the original change in spending that caused it."[32] Last year, some economists predicted that every dollar of debt funded government spending could magically lead to $2 or $3 of new private activity. The Obama administration said this when it promised 3 million jobs would be "saved or created" from its $787 billion stimulus package.[33]

To take advantage of the multiplier, countries were urged to throw fiscal caution to the wind. In its Economic Outlook published in November 2008, the IMF, which is the international agency whose mission is to prevent economic panics, advised member nations like Greece: "There is a clear need for additional macroeconomic policy stimulus relative to what has been announced thus far, to support growth and provide a context

Figure 16 | Education and Medical Prices Skyrocket while Import Prices Drop
(Percent Change, 2000-2009)

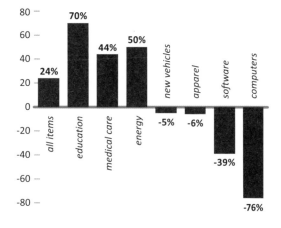

Source: U.S. Bureau of Labor Statistics

to restore health to financial sectors."[34] At its February 2009, emergency "Group of 20" meetings, the IMF economists advised "aggressive" pedal-to-the-metal government spending "to resolve the crisis."[35] The IMF continued that "a key feature of a fiscal stimulus program is that it should support demand for a *prolonged period of time* and be applied broadly across countries" (emphasis added).[36] IMF officials also lectured that the global risk was that government borrowing would be too small, not too large.

The United States, Germany, France, Ireland, Spain, and almost all OECD countries took that advice to heart, but perhaps none more so than Greece, which employed Keynesianism on steroids. In 2009, Greek debt as a share of GDP skyrocketed to 125 percent of GDP from an already high 109 percent in 2008[37] as the socialist government promised voters more public sector hiring, more generous benefits and more subsidies to ailing industries.[38]

Most of the other nations in Europe that are on the potential contamination list—Ireland, Italy, Portugal and Spain—also dutifully passed textbook Keynesian spending stimulus plans and their debt-to-GDP levels also soared. In 2010, Italian debt hit 118 percent of GDP, and Portuguese debt is nearly 90 percent and climbing. Spain's 2009 deficit soared to 11 percent of GDP and Ireland's to 14 percent.[39] Just what the Keynesian doctors ordered.

Now Greece's unemployment is rising rapidly, output has crashed, and interest rates are rising as its sovereign debt has been classified as toxic. Keynesian economics has gone haywire. The rapid deterioration of Greek debt is a painful but useful lesson that debt financing of runaway government spending is anything but free and hardly something to worry about, as Lord Keynes himself famously put it, only "in the long run" when "we are all dead."[40] Instead, what we are witnessing in Greece is that runaway government spending can derail a national economy with the suddenness and ferocity of a thunderbolt. Mr. Keynes and his disciples never counted on the punishing force of modern-day bond vigilantes.

Now we have an astonishing twist in the story. The new "emergency" rescue plan imposed on Greece concocted by many of the same economists who advised that nation to spend, spend, spend just 18 months ago, is centered around "austerity."

The IMF and European Union have commanded Greece to cut government budgets, slash pensions and payrolls, and raise the value-added tax from 19 percent at the start of the year to 21 or even 23 percent, to forestall a financial meltdown.[41] In other words, never mind our earlier counsel to run up the credit card; what is needed now is less debt and less consumption and demand. Huh? The politicians in Greece, all of Europe, and here in the United States, can be excused for complaining of policy whiplash from the contradictory advice they are getting from Keynesian scholars.

Some of the Keynesians are now seeking—as they watch the destructive consequences brought on by their own dismal advice of 2008 and 2009—an abandonment or devaluation of the euro so debt deluged countries like Greece can repay or repudiate their sovereign debt. Of course, a currency revaluation will only incite inflation, as we should have learned in the 1970s, and cause rapid acceleration in interest rates on government bonds, making this solution self-defeating at best. The experiences of Argentina, Bolivia, and Mexico should have taught that lesson.

Keynesians defend their contradictory advice by explaining that what they meant for countries like Greece, Ireland, Portugal, and the United States was temporary debt fueled government stimulus followed by medium term progress to restore balanced budgets. But even if plausible in theory, this has always been a fantasy in the real world. Giving politicians like Nancy Pelosi and Gordon Brown the green light to spend money irresponsibly is like giving a pyromaniac a blow torch. In Washington, D.C. and European capitals, government spending programs are never temporary.

The U.S. Congress still has not ended stimulus programs that date back to the New Deal era of the 1930s, and already stimulus plans from 2009 are being extended. Keynesianism has always been an intellectual hoax, an excuse to ratchet up the government's reach and to redistribute income in the here and now, while paying the bills later by raising taxes. All under the assumption that there are no negative multiplier effects to tax increases.

Keynesianism is also crumbling before our very eyes because the promised recovery in jobs in the United States and Europe simply has not materialized. The economic rebound in Europe from colossal government borrowing has only brought on a new round of financial turmoil. The countries with the most debt are getting clobbered in global markets as capital flees from them. Japan, since 1991, should have been the showcase for the Keynesian canard, as the Japanese government has unsuccessfully launched at least five "stimulus" plans over the past 20 years while its stock market has lost two-thirds of its value. Even the Obama administration was forced to concede that its stimulus was a failure: agreeing to extend supply-side tax rate cuts at the end of 2010 was an admission that stimulus spending had failed.

The Keynesian response to the observable failures of its policies is to call for even more stimulus, except, of course, when the stimulus is too much—as in Greece. What does the United States have to show from its stimulus folly? All of $3 trillion of new debt and no new jobs.

John Maynard Keynes once famously declared that politicians who pursue wrong-headed policy prescriptions "are usually the slave of some defunct economist."[42] The defunct and derailed idea of Keynesianism is at the center of the panic in Europe. It threatens to shift the U.S. economy into a lower gear for years to come. Its application has placed governments across the globe in deeper levels of debt than they have experienced any time since the end of World War II. The global capital markets won't tolerate this much longer,

and even the Keynesians of Europe are recognizing that reality. But will U.S. politicians in the states, cities, and Washington turn away from this failed policy?

Conclusion

Increasing spending, bailing out failing firms, increasing tax rates, and printing money have all been discredited as ways to create growth or balance a budget. These fool's gold tactics and the policies of borrowing and spending will work no better in state capitals than they did in Washington. So what has worked in the past to generate jobs and prosperity?

Real and sustainable economic growth is generated by creating incentives for businesses to compete and to discover the most efficient ways to provide goods and services consumers demand. Government subsidies only distort this competitive process. It is neither pro-business nor pro-growth to give special handouts to one industry or another. The principles for prosperity are simple and timeless: promote economic freedom. Do this by keeping taxes low, operating based on a lean and efficient budget that neither wastes money nor provides unwarranted subsidies, and minimizing regulation. States focused on these principles will benefit from economic growth and prosperity.

ENDNOTES

1   Isidore, Chris. "Stimulus Price Tag: $2.8 Trillion." *CNN Money.* December 20, 2010.

2   Paletta, Damian. "U.S. Debt Nears Ceiling, Hits Record $14.21786 Trillion." *The Wall Street Journal.* April 4, 2011.

3   U.S. Bureau of Labor Statistics.

4   Priebus, Reince. "Happy Stimulus Day: How's That Working Out for You?" *The Washington Times.* February 16, 2011.

5   "Pelosi's Mouse Slated for $30M Slice of Cheese." *The Washington Times.* February 12, 2009.

6   "Requirements and Procedures for Consumer Assistance to Recycle and Save Program." U.S. Department of Transportation. July 29, 2009.

7   Stossel, John. "Economic Illiterates in Washington." *RealClearPolitics.* September 2, 2009.

8   Mourdock, Richard. Testimony before the Congressional Oversight Panel. July 27, 2009.

9   "Eyes on the Fed: Read the Fed Statement." *CNN Money.* November 3, 2010.

10   Goldman, David. "Follow the Money: Bailout Tracker." *CNN Money.* April 6, 2009.

11   Reed, Lawrence. "Great Myths of the Great Depression." Mackinac Center for Public Policy. 2008.

12 *Ibid.*

13 Beach, William. "We're Spending More Than Ever and It Doesn't Work." The Heritage Foundation. January 14, 2009.

14 Shlaes, Amity. "The Forgotten Man." HarperCollins. 2007.

15 McIntyre, Ken. "Tax Cuts for Investors, Not Massive Spending, Creates Jobs." The Heritage Foundation. January 7, 2009.

16 "Japan's Lost Decade." *The Economist*. September 26, 2002.

17 U.S. Federal Reserve Board. "Flow of Funds Accounts of the United States: Historical Data." December 9, 2010.

18 The president did sign an extension of the Bush tax cuts in December 2010, which will help the economy in 2011 and 2012, but these are primarily temporary extensions of current rates, not tax rate cuts.

19 Kim, Anthony, et al. "2011 Index of Economic Freedom." The Heritage Foundation. January 12, 2011.

20 Carlsson, Fredrik and Lundström, Susanna. "The Effects of Economic and Political Freedom on CO2 Emmissions." Göteborg University. February 2003.

    Also see: Barrett, Scott and Graddy, Kathryn. "Freedom, growth, and the environment." Environment and Development Economics. Cambridge University Press, vol. 5(04), pages 433-456. October 2000.

21 Tax Foundation. "Facts and Figures on Government Finance." 38th edition. 2004.

22 Laffer, Arthur B., Moore, Stephen and Tanous, Peter J. "The End of Prosperity." Simon & Schuster. 2008.

23 *Ibid.*

24 Moore, Stephen. "Remembering the Real Economic Legacy of JFK." *Human Events*. May 19, 2003.

25 Chen, Duanjie and Mintz, Jack. "New Estimates of Effective Corporate Tax Rates on Business Investment." Cato Institute. February 2011.

26 Economic Recovery Advisory Board. "The Report on Tax Reform Options: Simplification, Compliance, and Corporate Taxation." August 2010.

27 U.S. Bureau of Economic Analysis.

28 U.S. Bureau of Labor Statistics.

29 White, Gregory. "Europe Just Pumped Up Its Bailout Fund to €700 Billion, but It's Not All Good News for Bond Holders." *Business Insider*. March 22, 2011.

30 Riedl, Brian. "Why Government Spending Does Not Stimulate Economic Growth: Answering the Critics." Heritage Foundation Backgrounder on Economy and Federal Budget. January 5, 2010.

31 Krugman, Paul. "Ideas for Obama." *The New York Times*. January 11, 2009. See also, "Economists Urge Fast Action on Stimulus." *The Wall Street Journal*. January 7, 2009.

32 Blinder, Alan S. "Keynesian Economics." *The Concise Encyclopedia of Economics*, 2nd ed. Library of Economics and Liberty. 2007.

33 De Rugy, Veronique. "Three Million Jobs: Really?" *National Review*. July 14, 2010.

34 International Monetary Fund. "IMF Urges Stimulus as Global Growth Marked Down Sharply." *IMF Survey Magazine*. November 6, 2008.

35 IMF. "IMF Urges G-20 States to Take More Decisive Action to Combat Crisis." *IMF Survey Magazine*. February 5, 2009.

36 *Ibid.*

37 Organization for Economic Development and Cooperation (OECD).

38 Dubois, Shelley. "Why cutting Greece's 14th Salary Payment is a bad idea." *CNN Money*. March 4, 2010.

39 "Eurostat New Cronos." ESDS International. April 7, 2011.

40 Keynes, John Maynard. "A Tract on Monetary Reform." 1923.

41 "Greece's Economic Woes." *The Economist*. April 7, 2011. See also, "Greece in Second 2% VAT Increase to 23%." TMF Group. May 2, 2010.

42 Keynes, John Maynard. "The General Theory of Employment Interest and Money." Palgrave Macmillan. 1935.

Seattle, Washington

State Rankings

State Rankings

The Economic Outlook Ranking is a forecast based on a state's current standing in 15 state policy variables. Each of these factors is influenced directly by state lawmakers through the legislative process. Generally speaking, states that spend less—especially on income transfer programs, and states that tax less—particularly on productive activities such as working or investing—experience higher growth rates than states which tax and spend more.

The Economic Performance Ranking is a backward-looking measure based on a state's performance on three important variables: Personal Income Per Capita, Absolute Domestic Migration, and Non-Farm Payroll Employment—all of which are highly influenced by state policy. This ranking details states' individual performances over the past 10 years based on this economic data.

Table 7 | ALEC-Laffer State Economic Outlook Rankings, 2011
Based upon equal-weighting of each state's rank in 15 policy variables

Rank	State	Rank	State
1	Utah	26	North Carolina
2	South Dakota	27	Kansas
3	Virginia	28	New Hampshire
4	Wyoming	29	Alaska
5	Idaho	30	Wisconsin
6	Colorado	31	West Virginia
7	North Dakota	32	Nebraska
8	Tennessee	33	Washington
9	Missouri	34	Delaware
10	Florida	35	Connecticut
11	Georgia	36	Montana
12	Arizona	37	Minnesota
13	Arkansas	38	Ohio
14	Oklahoma	39	New Mexico
15	Louisiana	40	Kentucky
16	Indiana	41	Pennsylvania
17	Nevada	42	Rhode Island
18	Texas	43	Oregon
19	Mississippi	44	Illinois
20	Alabama	45	New Jersey
21	Maryland	46	Hawaii
22	South Carolina	47	California
23	Iowa	48	Maine
24	Massachusetts	49	Vermont
25	Michigan	50	New York

Table 8 | ALEC-Laffer State Economic Performance Rankings, 1999-2009

Rank	State	Absolute Domestic Migration	Personal Income Per Capita	Non-Farm Payroll Employment
1	Wyoming	25	1	1
2	Texas	2	21	7
3	Montana	20	4	8
4	North Dakota	31	2	3
5	New Mexico	23	6	9
6	Virginia	12	15	13
7	Alaska	29	9	2
8	Florida	1	25	15
9	Oklahoma	21	5	17
10	Arkansas	16	11	22
11	South Dakota	27	10	12
12	Hawaii	33	7	11
13	Washington	9	30	14
14	Utah	17	32	5
15	Arizona	3	42	10
16	West Virginia	26	8	21
17	Idaho	13	39	6
18	Nevada	6	49	4
19	Vermont	28	14	24
20	Maine	24	18	29
21	Maryland	41	12	18
22	North Carolina	4	45	23
23	Alabama	14	19	40
24	Colorado	10	44	19
25	South Carolina	7	31	36
26	Nebraska	35	23	16
27	Louisiana	43	3	32
28	Iowa	38	17	25
29	New Hampshire	22	38	20
30	Oregon	11	43	27
31	Kentucky	15	29	38
32	Delaware	18	33	33
33	Georgia	5	48	35
34	Kansas	40	20	28
35	Rhode Island	36	13	43
36	Tennessee	8	41	45
37	Pennsylvania	39	24	31
38	Missouri	19	37	39
39	Mississippi	34	16	46
40	New York	50	22	26
41	Minnesota	37	36	30
42	New Jersey	46	27	34
43	Connecticut	42	26	42
44	Wisconsin	30	40	41
45	Massachusetts	44	28	44
46	California	49	35	37
47	Indiana	32	46	48
48	Illinois	48	34	47
49	Ohio	45	47	49
50	Michigan	47	50	50

Alabama

23 Economic Performance Rank

20 Economic Outlook Rank

Economic Performance Rank (1=best 50=worst)
A historical measure based on a state's performance (equally weighted average) in the three important performance variables shown below. These variables are highly influenced by state policy.

Economic Outlook Rank (1=best 50=worst)
A forecast based on a state's standing (equally weighted average) in the 15 important state policy variables shown below. Data reflect state + local rates and revenues and any effect of federal deductibility.

Personal Income Per Capita
Cumulative Growth 1999-2009   **43.5%   Rank: 19**

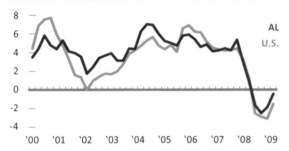

Absolute Domestic Migration
Cumulative 2000-2009   **86,287   Rank: 14**

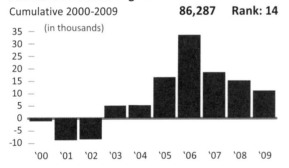

Non-Farm Payroll Employment
Cumulative Growth 1999-2009   **-3.1%   Rank: 40**

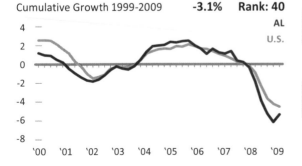

Historical Ranking Comparison	2008	2009	2010
ECONOMIC OUTLOOK RANK	**15**	**16**	**17**

Variable	Data	Rank
Top Marginal Personal Income Tax Rate	4.25%	11
Top Marginal Corporate Income Tax Rate	4.23%	5
Personal Income Tax Progressivity (change in tax liability per $1,000 of income)	-$1.51	1
Property Tax Burden (per $1,000 of personal income)	$14.77	1
Sales Tax Burden (per $1,000 of personal income)	$26.56	31
Remaining Tax Burden (per $1,000 of personal income)	$22.86	41
Estate/Inheritance Tax Levied?	No	1
Recently Legislated Tax Changes (2009 & 2010, per $1,000 of personal income)	-$1.79	27
Debt Service as a Share of Tax Revenue	7.6%	21
Public Employees Per 10,000 of Population (full-time equivalent)	607.5	40
State Liability System Survey (tort litigation treatment, judicial impartiality, etc.)	45.5	47
State Minimum Wage (federal floor is $7.25)	$7.25	1
Average Workers' Compensation Costs (per $100 of payroll)	$2.45	41
Right-to-Work State? (option to join or support a union)	Yes	1
Number of Tax Expenditure Limits (0= least/worst 3=most/best)	0	35

Alaska

7 Economic Performance Rank

29 Economic Outlook Rank

Economic Performance Rank (1=best 50=worst)
A historical measure based on a state's performance (equally weighted average) in the three important performance variables shown below. These variables are highly influenced by state policy.

Economic Outlook Rank (1=best 50=worst)
A forecast based on a state's standing (equally weighted average) in the 15 important state policy variables shown below. Data reflect state + local rates and revenues and any effect of federal deductibility.

Personal Income Per Capita
Cumulative Growth 1999-2009   **50.0%   Rank: 9**

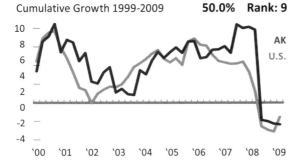

Absolute Domestic Migration   -7,829   Rank: 29
Cumulative 2000-2009

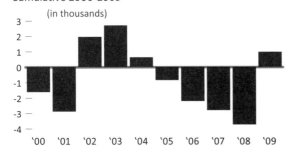

Non-Farm Payroll Employment
Cumulative Growth 1999-2009   **15.0%   Rank: 2**

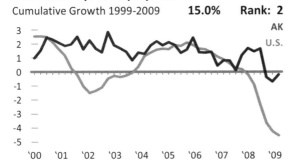

Historical Ranking Comparison	2008	2009	2010
ECONOMIC OUTLOOK RANK	**37**	**38**	**22**

Variable	Data	Rank
Top Marginal Personal Income Tax Rate	0.00%	1
Top Marginal Corporate Income Tax Rate	9.40%	43
Personal Income Tax Progressivity (change in tax liability per $1,000 of income)	$0.00	2
Property Tax Burden (per $1,000 of personal income)	$36.39	38
Sales Tax Burden (per $1,000 of personal income)	$7.31	5
Remaining Tax Burden (per $1,000 of personal income)	$18.02	25
Estate/Inheritance Tax Levied?	No	1
Recently Legislated Tax Changes (2009 & 2010, per $1,000 of personal income)	-$2.42	25
Debt Service as a Share of Tax Revenue	4.8%	2
Public Employees Per 10,000 of Population (full-time equivalent)	765.2	49
State Liability System Survey (tort litigation treatment, judicial impartiality, etc.)	56.6	33
State Minimum Wage (federal floor is $7.25)	$7.75	42
Average Workers' Compensation Costs (per $100 of payroll)	$3.10	49
Right-to-Work State? (option to join or support a union)	No	50
Number of Tax Expenditure Limits (0= least/worst 3=most/best)	1	13

Arizona

15 Economic Performance Rank

12 Economic Outlook Rank

Economic Performance Rank (1=best 50=worst)
A historical measure based on a state's performance (equally weighted average) in the three important performance variables shown below. These variables are highly influenced by state policy.

Economic Outlook Rank (1=best 50=worst)
A forecast based on a state's standing (equally weighted average) in the 15 important state policy variables shown below. Data reflect state + local rates and revenues and any effect of federal deductibility.

Personal Income Per Capita
Cumulative Growth 1999-2009   **32.6%**   **Rank: 42**

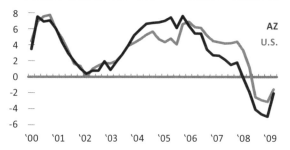

Absolute Domestic Migration
Cumulative 2000-2009   **731,883**   **Rank: 3**
(in thousands)

Non-Farm Payroll Employment
Cumulative Growth 1999-2009   **8.9%**   **Rank: 10**

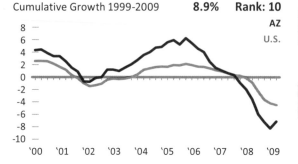

Historical Ranking Comparison	2008	2009	2010
ECONOMIC OUTLOOK RANK	**6**	**3**	**3**

Variable	Data	Rank
Top Marginal Personal Income Tax Rate	4.54%	13
Top Marginal Corporate Income Tax Rate	6.97%	24
Personal Income Tax Progressivity (change in tax liability per $1,000 of income)	$10.49	34
Property Tax Burden (per $1,000 of personal income)	$30.10	23
Sales Tax Burden (per $1,000 of personal income)	$40.89	45
Remaining Tax Burden (per $1,000 of personal income)	$13.10	5
Estate/Inheritance Tax Levied?	No	1
Recently Legislated Tax Changes (2009 & 2010, per $1,000 of personal income)	$0.85	37
Debt Service as a Share of Tax Revenue	8.5%	32
Public Employees Per 10,000 of Population (full-time equivalent)	463.3	2
State Liability System Survey (tort litigation treatment, judicial impartiality, etc.)	65.0	13
State Minimum Wage (federal floor is $7.25)	$7.35	34
Average Workers' Compensation Costs (per $100 of payroll)	$1.71	13
Right-to-Work State? (option to join or support a union)	Yes	1
Number of Tax Expenditure Limits (0= least/worst 3=most/best)	2	4

Arkansas

10 Economic Performance Rank

13 Economic Outlook Rank

Economic Performance Rank (1=best 50=worst)

A historical measure based on a state's performance (equally weighted average) in the three important performance variables shown below. These variables are highly influenced by state policy.

Economic Outlook Rank (1=best 50=worst)

A forecast based on a state's standing (equally weighted average) in the 15 important state policy variables shown below. Data reflect state + local rates and revenues and any effect of federal deductibility.

Personal Income Per Capita
Cumulative Growth 1999-2009 **48.9%** **Rank: 11**

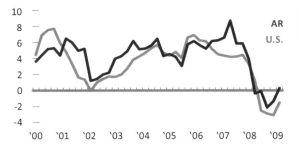

Absolute Domestic Migration
Cumulative 2000-2009 **75,358** **Rank: 16**
(in thousands)

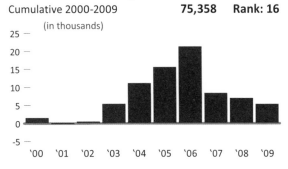

Non-Farm Payroll Employment
Cumulative Growth 1999-2009 **0.4%** **Rank: 22**

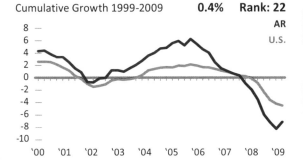

Historical Ranking Comparison	2008	2009	2010
ECONOMIC OUTLOOK RANK	11	12	13

Variable	Data	Rank
Top Marginal Personal Income Tax Rate	7.00%	33
Top Marginal Corporate Income Tax Rate	6.50%	20
Personal Income Tax Progressivity (change in tax liability per $1,000 of income)	$13.82	40
Property Tax Burden (per $1,000 of personal income)	$15.78	2
Sales Tax Burden (per $1,000 of personal income)	$40.09	43
Remaining Tax Burden (per $1,000 of personal income)	$16.07	12
Estate/Inheritance Tax Levied?	No	1
Recently Legislated Tax Changes (2009 & 2010, per $1,000 of personal income)	-$4.04	16
Debt Service as a Share of Tax Revenue	5.6%	4
Public Employees Per 10,000 of Population (full-time equivalent)	563.6	30
State Liability System Survey (tort litigation treatment, judicial impartiality, etc.)	48.7	44
State Minimum Wage (federal floor is $7.25)	$7.25	1
Average Workers' Compensation Costs (per $100 of payroll)	$1.18	3
Right-to-Work State? (option to join or support a union)	Yes	1
Number of Tax Expenditure Limits (0= least/worst 3=most/best)	1	13

California

46 Economic
Performance Rank

47 Economic
Outlook Rank

Economic Performance Rank (1=best 50=worst)

A historical measure based on a state's performance (equally weighted average) in the three important performance variables shown below. These variables are highly influenced by state policy.

Personal Income Per Capita

Cumulative Growth 1999-2009   **34.7%**   **Rank: 35**

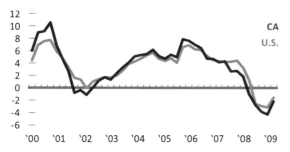

Absolute Domestic Migration

Cumulative 2000-2009   **-1,466,917**   **Rank: 49**

Non-Farm Payroll Employment

Cumulative Growth 1999-2009   **-2.3%**   **Rank: 37**

Economic Outlook Rank (1=best 50=worst)

A forecast based on a state's standing (equally weighted average) in the 15 important state policy variables shown below. Data reflect state + local rates and revenues and any effect of federal deductibility.

Historical Ranking Comparison

ECONOMIC OUTLOOK RANK	2008	2009	2010
	42	**43**	**46**

Variable	Data	Rank
Top Marginal Personal Income Tax Rate	10.30%	47
Top Marginal Corporate Income Tax Rate	8.84%	38
Personal Income Tax Progressivity (change in tax liability per $1,000 of income)	$36.15	50
Property Tax Burden (per $1,000 of personal income)	$33.03	31
Sales Tax Burden (per $1,000 of personal income)	$25.73	29
Remaining Tax Burden (per $1,000 of personal income)	$15.33	8
Estate/Inheritance Tax Levied?	No	1
Recently Legislated Tax Changes (2009 & 2010, per $1,000 of personal income)	$3.77	46
Debt Service as a Share of Tax Revenue	8.5%	31
Public Employees Per 10,000 of Population (full-time equivalent)	496.6	7
State Liability System Survey (tort litigation treatment, judicial impartiality, etc.)	47.2	46
State Minimum Wage (federal floor is $7.25)	$8.00	43
Average Workers' Compensation Costs (per $100 of payroll)	2.68	46
Right-to-Work State? (option to join or support a union)	No	50
Number of Tax Expenditure Limits (0= least/worst 3=most/best)	2	4

Colorado

24 Economic Performance Rank

6 Economic Outlook Rank

Economic Performance Rank (1=best 50=worst)
A historical measure based on a state's performance (equally weighted average) in the three important performance variables shown below. These variables are highly influenced by state policy.

Economic Outlook Rank (1=best 50=worst)
A forecast based on a state's standing (equally weighted average) in the 15 important state policy variables shown below. Data reflect state + local rates and revenues and any effect of federal deductibility.

Personal Income Per Capita
Cumulative Growth 1999-2009 **30.8%** **Rank: 44**

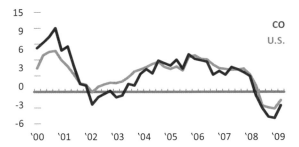

Absolute Domestic Migration
Cumulative 2000-2009 **203,700** **Rank: 10**
(in thousands)

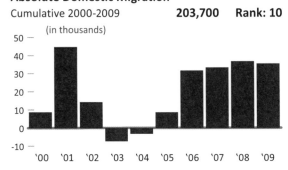

Non-Farm Payroll Employment
Cumulative Growth 1999-2009 **2.6%** **Rank: 19**

Historical Ranking Comparison	2008	2009	2010
ECONOMIC OUTLOOK RANK	**9**	**2**	**2**

Variable	Data	Rank
Top Marginal Personal Income Tax Rate	4.63%	14
Top Marginal Corporate Income Tax Rate	4.63%	6
Personal Income Tax Progressivity (change in tax liability per $1,000 of income)	$0.00	2
Property Tax Burden (per $1,000 of personal income)	$28.98	19
Sales Tax Burden (per $1,000 of personal income)	$24.86	28
Remaining Tax Burden (per $1,000 of personal income)	$11.83	3
Estate/Inheritance Tax Levied?	No	1
Recently Legislated Tax Changes (2009 & 2010, per $1,000 of personal income)	$0.93	38
Debt Service as a Share of Tax Revenue	11.1%	46
Public Employees Per 10,000 of Population (full-time equivalent)	549.0	26
State Liability System Survey (tort litigation treatment, judicial impartiality, etc.)	65.8	8
State Minimum Wage (federal floor is $7.25)	$7.36	36
Average Workers' Compensation Costs (per $100 of payroll)	$1.39	4
Right-to-Work State? (option to join or support a union)	No	50
Number of Tax Expenditure Limits (0= least/worst 3=most/best)	3	1

Connecticut

43 Economic Performance Rank

35 Economic Outlook Rank

Economic Performance Rank (1=best 50=worst)

A historical measure based on a state's performance (equally weighted average) in the three important performance variables shown below. These variables are highly influenced by state policy.

Economic Outlook Rank (1=best 50=worst)

A forecast based on a state's standing (equally weighted average) in the 15 important state policy variables shown below. Data reflect state + local rates and revenues and any effect of federal deductibility.

Personal Income Per Capita

Cumulative Growth 1999-2009 **39.6% Rank: 26**

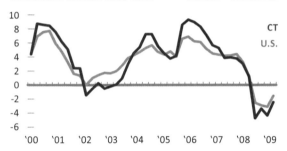

Historical Ranking Comparison	2008	2009	2010
ECONOMIC OUTLOOK RANK	**40**	**32**	**36**

Variable	Data	Rank
Top Marginal Personal Income Tax Rate	6.50%	27
Top Marginal Corporate Income Tax Rate	7.50%	26
Personal Income Tax Progressivity (change in tax liability per $1,000 of income)	$2.67	18
Property Tax Burden (per $1,000 of personal income)	$41.66	42
Sales Tax Burden (per $1,000 of personal income)	$17.74	11
Remaining Tax Burden (per $1,000 of personal income)	$15.61	10
Estate/Inheritance Tax Levied?	Yes	50
Recently Legislated Tax Changes (2009 & 2010, per $1,000 of personal income)	$1.00	39
Debt Service as a Share of Tax Revenue	7.1%	15
Public Employees Per 10,000 of Population (full-time equivalent)	531.1	16
State Liability System Survey (tort litigation treatment, judicial impartiality, etc.)	62.1	24
State Minimum Wage (federal floor is $7.25)	$8.25	46
Average Workers' Compensation Costs (per $100 of payroll)	$2.55	45
Right-to-Work State? (option to join or support a union)	No	50
Number of Tax Expenditure Limits (0= least/worst 3=most/best)	1	13

Absolute Domestic Migration

Cumulative 2000-2009 **-100,055 Rank: 42**

(in thousands)

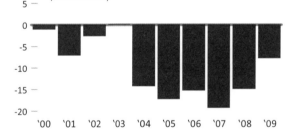

Non-Farm Payroll Employment

Cumulative Growth 1999-2009 **-3.8% Rank: 42**

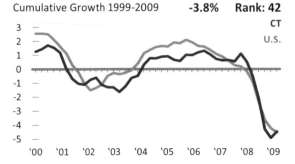

Delaware

32 Economic Performance Rank

34 Economic Outlook Rank

Economic Performance Rank (1=best 50=worst)

A historical measure based on a state's performance (equally weighted average) in the three important performance variables shown below. These variables are highly influenced by state policy.

Economic Outlook Rank (1=best 50=worst)

A forecast based on a state's standing (equally weighted average) in the 15 important state policy variables shown below. Data reflect state + local rates and revenues and any effect of federal deductibility.

Personal Income Per Capita

Cumulative Growth 1999-2009   **35.1%   Rank: 33**

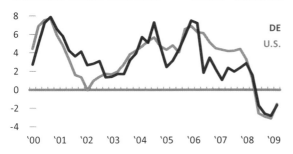

Historical Ranking Comparison	2008	2009	2010
ECONOMIC OUTLOOK RANK	**31**	**31**	**37**

Variable	Data	Rank
Top Marginal Personal Income Tax Rate	8.20%	42
Top Marginal Corporate Income Tax Rate	9.98%	47
Personal Income Tax Progressivity (change in tax liability per $1,000 of income)	$11.34	35
Property Tax Burden (per $1,000 of personal income)	$17.15	4
Sales Tax Burden (per $1,000 of personal income)	$0.00	1
Remaining Tax Burden (per $1,000 of personal income)	$31.64	49
Estate/Inheritance Tax Levied?	Yes	50
Recently Legislated Tax Changes (2009 & 2010, per $1,000 of personal income)	$9.38	49
Debt Service as a Share of Tax Revenue	9.2%	36
Public Employees Per 10,000 of Population (full-time equivalent)	548.5	25
State Liability System Survey (tort litigation treatment, judicial impartiality, etc.)	77.2	1
State Minimum Wage (federal floor is $7.25)	$7.25	1
Average Workers' Compensation Costs (per $100 of payroll)	$1.85	17
Right-to-Work State? (option to join or support a union)	No	50
Number of Tax Expenditure Limits (0= least/worst 3=most/best)	2	4

Absolute Domestic Migration

Cumulative 2000-2009   **46,411   Rank: 18**

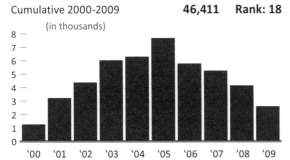

Non-Farm Payroll Employment

Cumulative Growth 1999-2009   **-1.7%   Rank: 33**

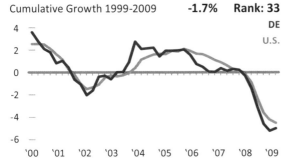

Florida

8 Economic
Performance Rank

10 Economic
Outlook Rank

Economic Performance Rank (1=best 50=worst)

A historical measure based on a state's performance (equally weighted average) in the three important performance variables shown below. These variables are highly influenced by state policy.

Economic Outlook Rank (1=best 50=worst)

A forecast based on a state's standing (equally weighted average) in the 15 important state policy variables shown below. Data reflect state + local rates and revenues and any effect of federal deductibility.

Personal Income Per Capita

Cumulative Growth 1999-2009 **40.1%** **Rank: 25**

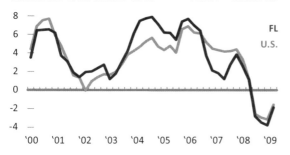

Absolute Domestic Migration

Cumulative 2000-2009 **1,281,521** **Rank: 1**

(in thousands)

Non-Farm Payroll Employment

Cumulative Growth 1999-2009 **3.9%** **Rank: 15**

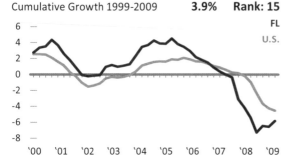

Historical Ranking Comparison	2008	2009	2010
ECONOMIC OUTLOOK RANK	**16**	**11**	**5**

Variable	Data	Rank
Top Marginal Personal Income Tax Rate	0.00%	1
Top Marginal Corporate Income Tax Rate	5.50%	13
Personal Income Tax Progressivity (change in tax liability per $1,000 of income)	$0.00	2
Property Tax Burden (per $1,000 of personal income)	$41.28	41
Sales Tax Burden (per $1,000 of personal income)	$31.18	39
Remaining Tax Burden (per $1,000 of personal income)	$24.22	43
Estate/Inheritance Tax Levied?	No	1
Recently Legislated Tax Changes (2009 & 2010, per $1,000 of personal income)	-$0.86	32
Debt Service as a Share of Tax Revenue	8.0%	27
Public Employees Per 10,000 of Population (full-time equivalent)	476.1	5
State Liability System Survey (tort litigation treatment, judicial impartiality, etc.)	53.9	41
State Minimum Wage (federal floor is $7.25)	$7.25	1
Average Workers' Compensation Costs (per $100 of payroll)	$1.70	11
Right-to-Work State? (option to join or support a union)	Yes	1
Number of Tax Expenditure Limits (0= least/worst 3=most/best)	2	4

Georgia

33 Economic Performance Rank

11 Economic Outlook Rank

Economic Performance Rank (1=best 50=worst)

A historical measure based on a state's performance (equally weighted average) in the three important performance variables shown below. These variables are highly influenced by state policy.

Economic Outlook Rank (1=best 50=worst)

A forecast based on a state's standing (equally weighted average) in the 15 important state policy variables shown below. Data reflect state + local rates and revenues and any effect of federal deductibility.

Personal Income Per Capita
Cumulative Growth 1999-2009 **24.0% Rank: 48**

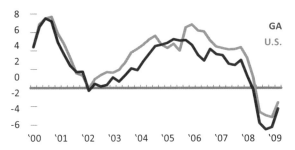

Absolute Domestic Migration
Cumulative 2000-2009 **569,651 Rank: 5**

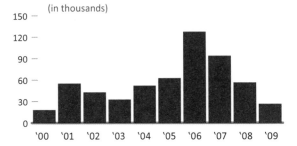

Non-Farm Payroll Employment
Cumulative Growth 1999-2009 **-2.0% Rank: 35**

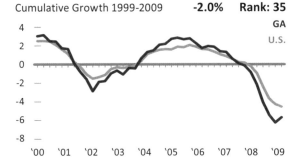

Historical Ranking Comparison	2008	2009	2010
ECONOMIC OUTLOOK RANK	**8**	**8**	**9**

Variable	Data	Rank
Top Marginal Personal Income Tax Rate	6.00%	25
Top Marginal Corporate Income Tax Rate	6.00%	16
Personal Income Tax Progressivity (change in tax liability per $1,000 of income)	$6.53	26
Property Tax Burden (per $1,000 of personal income)	$30.25	24
Sales Tax Burden (per $1,000 of personal income)	$28.92	36
Remaining Tax Burden (per $1,000 of personal income)	$11.31	2
Estate/Inheritance Tax Levied?	No	1
Recently Legislated Tax Changes (2009 & 2010, per $1,000 of personal income)	-$3.82	18
Debt Service as a Share of Tax Revenue	5.7%	5
Public Employees Per 10,000 of Population (full-time equivalent)	538.7	20
State Liability System Survey (tort litigation treatment, judicial impartiality, etc.)	60.9	27
State Minimum Wage (federal floor is $7.25)	$7.25	1
Average Workers' Compensation Costs (per $100 of payroll)	$2.08	27
Right-to-Work State? (option to join or support a union)	Yes	1
Number of Tax Expenditure Limits (0= least/worst 3=most/best)	0	35

Hawaii

12 Economic Performance Rank

46 Economic Outlook Rank

Economic Performance Rank (1=best 50=worst)
A historical measure based on a state's performance (equally weighted average) in the three important performance variables shown below. These variables are highly influenced by state policy.

Economic Outlook Rank (1=best 50=worst)
A forecast based on a state's standing (equally weighted average) in the 15 important state policy variables shown below. Data reflect state + local rates and revenues and any effect of federal deductibility.

Personal Income Per Capita
Cumulative Growth 1999-2009   **50.7%**   **Rank: 7**

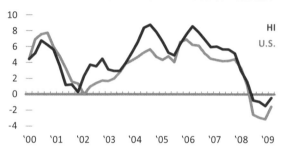

Absolute Domestic Migration
Cumulative 2000-2009   **-29,113**   **Rank: 33**

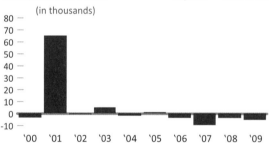

Non-Farm Payroll Employment
Cumulative Growth 1999-2009   **8.6%**   **Rank: 11**

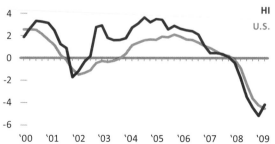

Historical Ranking Comparison	2008	2009	2010
ECONOMIC OUTLOOK RANK	**41**	**41**	**39**

Variable	Data	Rank
Top Marginal Personal Income Tax Rate	11.00%	48
Top Marginal Corporate Income Tax Rate	6.40%	19
Personal Income Tax Progressivity (change in tax liability per $1,000 of income)	$13.22	38
Property Tax Burden (per $1,000 of personal income)	$23.23	10
Sales Tax Burden (per $1,000 of personal income)	$48.56	49
Remaining Tax Burden (per $1,000 of personal income)	$22.47	40
Estate/Inheritance Tax Levied?	Yes	50
Recently Legislated Tax Changes (2009 & 2010, per $1,000 of personal income)	$3.48	45
Debt Service as a Share of Tax Revenue	9.4%	38
Public Employees Per 10,000 of Population (full-time equivalent)	582.5	35
State Liability System Survey (tort litigation treatment, judicial impartiality, etc.)	56.4	35
State Minimum Wage (federal floor is $7.25)	$7.25	1
Average Workers' Compensation Costs (per $100 of payroll)	$1.70	11
Right-to-Work State? (option to join or support a union)	No	50
Number of Tax Expenditure Limits (0= least/worst 3=most/best)	1	13

Idaho

17 Economic Performance Rank

5 Economic Outlook Rank

Economic Performance Rank (1=best 50=worst)
A historical measure based on a state's performance (equally weighted average) in the three important performance variables shown below. These variables are highly influenced by state policy.

Economic Outlook Rank (1=best 50=worst)
A forecast based on a state's standing (equally weighted average) in the 15 important state policy variables shown below. Data reflect state + local rates and revenues and any effect of federal deductibility.

Personal Income Per Capita
Cumulative Growth 1999-2009   **33.4%**   **Rank: 39**

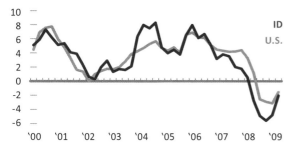

Absolute Domestic Migration
Cumulative 2000-2009   **114,914**   **Rank: 13**

(in thousands)

Non-Farm Payroll Employment
Cumulative Growth 1999-2009   **10.7%**   **Rank: 6**

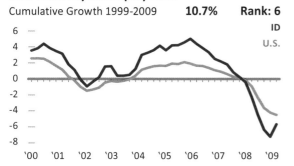

Historical Ranking Comparison	2008	2009	2010
ECONOMIC OUTLOOK RANK	**10**	**14**	**7**

Variable	Data	Rank
Top Marginal Personal Income Tax Rate	7.80%	38
Top Marginal Corporate Income Tax Rate	7.60%	27
Personal Income Tax Progressivity (change in tax liability per $1,000 of income)	$14.17	41
Property Tax Burden (per $1,000 of personal income)	$23.56	11
Sales Tax Burden (per $1,000 of personal income)	$26.90	33
Remaining Tax Burden (per $1,000 of personal income)	$15.45	9
Estate/Inheritance Tax Levied?	No	1
Recently Legislated Tax Changes (2009 & 2010, per $1,000 of personal income)	-$4.73	5
Debt Service as a Share of Tax Revenue	5.4%	3
Public Employees Per 10,000 of Population (full-time equivalent)	509.9	11
State Liability System Survey (tort litigation treatment, judicial impartiality, etc.)	63.9	18
State Minimum Wage (federal floor is $7.25)	$7.25	1
Average Workers' Compensation Costs (per $100 of payroll)	$1.98	22
Right-to-Work State? (option to join or support a union)	Yes	1
Number of Tax Expenditure Limits (0= least/worst 3=most/best)	1	13

Illinois

48 Economic Performance Rank

44 Economic Outlook Rank

Economic Performance Rank (1=best 50=worst)

A historical measure based on a state's performance (equally weighted average) in the three important performance variables shown below. These variables are highly influenced by state policy.

Economic Outlook Rank (1=best 50=worst)

A forecast based on a state's standing (equally weighted average) in the 15 important state policy variables shown below. Data reflect state + local rates and revenues and any effect of federal deductibility.

Personal Income Per Capita

Cumulative Growth 1999-2009   **34.8%   Rank: 34**

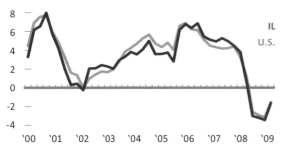

Historical Ranking Comparison	2008	2009	2010
ECONOMIC OUTLOOK RANK	**43**	**44**	**47**

Variable	Data	Rank
Top Marginal Personal Income Tax Rate	5.00%	17
Top Marginal Corporate Income Tax Rate	9.50%	44
Personal Income Tax Progressivity (change in tax liability per $1,000 of income)	$0.80	16
Property Tax Burden (per $1,000 of personal income)	$38.91	39
Sales Tax Burden (per $1,000 of personal income)	$17.01	10
Remaining Tax Burden (per $1,000 of personal income)	$24.78	45
Estate/Inheritance Tax Levied?	No	1
Recently Legislated Tax Changes (2009 & 2010, per $1,000 of personal income)	-$4.08	14
Debt Service as a Share of Tax Revenue	9.8%	42
Public Employees Per 10,000 of Population (full-time equivalent)	497.8	9
State Liability System Survey (tort litigation treatment, judicial impartiality, etc.)	47.9	45
State Minimum Wage (federal floor is $7.25)	$8.25	46
Average Workers' Compensation Costs (per $100 of payroll)	$3.05	48
Right-to-Work State? (option to join or support a union)	No	50
Number of Tax Expenditure Limits (0= least/worst 3=most/best)	0	35

Absolute Domestic Migration

Cumulative 2000-2009   **-652,205   Rank: 48**

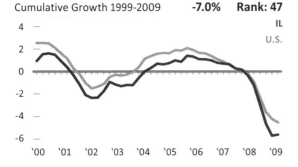

Non-Farm Payroll Employment

Cumulative Growth 1999-2009   **-7.0%   Rank: 47**

Indiana

47 Economic Performance Rank

16 Economic Outlook Rank

Economic Performance Rank (1=best 50=worst)

A historical measure based on a state's performance (equally weighted average) in the three important performance variables shown below. These variables are highly influenced by state policy.

Personal Income Per Capita

Cumulative Growth 1999-2009   **28.7%**   **Rank: 46**

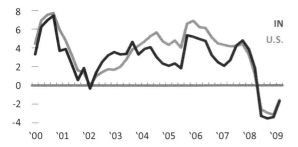

Absolute Domestic Migration

Cumulative 2000-2009   **-25,006**   **Rank: 32**

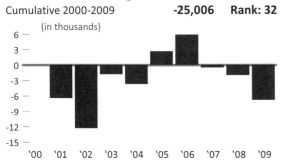

Non-Farm Payroll Employment

Cumulative Growth 1999-2009   **-7.7%**   **Rank: 48**

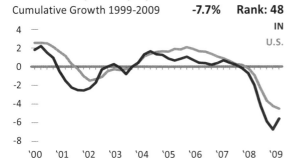

Economic Outlook Rank (1=best 50=worst)

A forecast based on a state's standing (equally weighted average) in the 15 important state policy variables shown below. Data reflect state + local rates and revenues and any effect of federal deductibility.

Historical Ranking Comparison	2008	2009	2010
ECONOMIC OUTLOOK RANK	12	17	20

Variable	Data	Rank
Top Marginal Personal Income Tax Rate	4.30%	12
Top Marginal Corporate Income Tax Rate	8.50%	34
Personal Income Tax Progressivity (change in tax liability per $1,000 of income)	$0.57	15
Property Tax Burden (per $1,000 of personal income)	$31.58	29
Sales Tax Burden (per $1,000 of personal income)	$26.13	30
Remaining Tax Burden (per $1,000 of personal income)	$18.13	27
Estate/Inheritance Tax Levied?	Yes	50
Recently Legislated Tax Changes (2009 & 2010, per $1,000 of personal income)	-$1.65	29
Debt Service as a Share of Tax Revenue	7.8%	26
Public Employees Per 10,000 of Population (full-time equivalent)	537.9	19
State Liability System Survey (tort litigation treatment, judicial impartiality, etc.)	69.9	3
State Minimum Wage (federal floor is $7.25)	$7.25	1
Average Workers' Compensation Costs (per $100 of payroll)	$1.16	2
Right-to-Work State? (option to join or support a union)	No	50
Number of Tax Expenditure Limits (0= least/worst 3=most/best)	1	13

Iowa

28 Economic Performance Rank

23 Economic Outlook Rank

Economic Performance Rank (1=best 50=worst)
A historical measure based on a state's performance (equally weighted average) in the three important performance variables shown below. These variables are highly influenced by state policy.

Economic Outlook Rank (1=best 50=worst)
A forecast based on a state's standing (equally weighted average) in the 15 important state policy variables shown below. Data reflect state + local rates and revenues and any effect of federal deductibility.

Personal Income Per Capita
Cumulative Growth 1999-2009   **44.4%**   **Rank: 17**

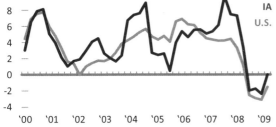

Absolute Domestic Migration
Cumulative 2000-2009   **-51,500**   **Rank: 38**

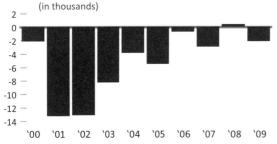

Non-Farm Payroll Employment
Cumulative Growth 1999-2009   **-0.5%**   **Rank: 25**

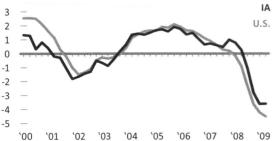

Historical Ranking Comparison	2008	2009	2010
ECONOMIC OUTLOOK RANK	**25**	**35**	**28**

Variable	Data	Rank
Top Marginal Personal Income Tax Rate	5.84%	23
Top Marginal Corporate Income Tax Rate	9.90%	46
Personal Income Tax Progressivity (change in tax liability per $1,000 of income)	$12.39	36
Property Tax Burden (per $1,000 of personal income)	$33.27	32
Sales Tax Burden (per $1,000 of personal income)	$21.75	20
Remaining Tax Burden (per $1,000 of personal income)	$18.54	30
Estate/Inheritance Tax Levied?	Yes	50
Recently Legislated Tax Changes (2009 & 2010, per $1,000 of personal income)	-$3.72	19
Debt Service as a Share of Tax Revenue	6.4%	10
Public Employees Per 10,000 of Population (full-time equivalent)	596.8	39
State Liability System Survey (tort litigation treatment, judicial impartiality, etc.)	69.4	5
State Minimum Wage (federal floor is $7.25)	$7.25	1
Average Workers' Compensation Costs (per $100 of payroll)	$1.82	15
Right-to-Work State? (option to join or support a union)	Yes	1
Number of Tax Expenditure Limits (0= least/worst 3=most/best)	1	13

Kansas

34 Economic Performance Rank

27 Economic Outlook Rank

Economic Performance Rank (1=best 50=worst)
A historical measure based on a state's performance (equally weighted average) in the three important performance variables shown below. These variables are highly influenced by state policy.

Economic Outlook Rank (1=best 50=worst)
A forecast based on a state's standing (equally weighted average) in the 15 important state policy variables shown below. Data reflect state + local rates and revenues and any effect of federal deductibility.

Personal Income Per Capita
Cumulative Growth 1999-2009 **43.0% Rank: 20**

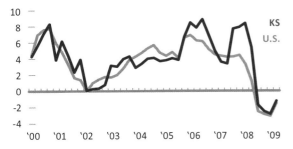

Absolute Domestic Migration
Cumulative 2000-2009 **-68,529 Rank: 40**

Non-Farm Payroll Employment
Cumulative Growth 1999-2009 **-0.6% Rank: 28**

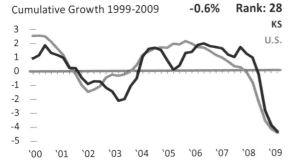

Historical Ranking Comparison	2008	2009	2010
ECONOMIC OUTLOOK RANK	**29**	**24**	**25**

Variable	Data	Rank
Top Marginal Personal Income Tax Rate	6.45%	26
Top Marginal Corporate Income Tax Rate	7.05%	25
Personal Income Tax Progressivity (change in tax liability per $1,000 of income)	$16.51	44
Property Tax Burden (per $1,000 of personal income)	$33.83	33
Sales Tax Burden (per $1,000 of personal income)	$28.07	35
Remaining Tax Burden (per $1,000 of personal income)	$13.13	6
Estate/Inheritance Tax Levied?	No	1
Recently Legislated Tax Changes (2009 & 2010, per $1,000 of personal income)	-$2.06	26
Debt Service as a Share of Tax Revenue	8.4%	30
Public Employees Per 10,000 of Population (full-time equivalent)	717.4	48
State Liability System Survey (tort litigation treatment, judicial impartiality, etc.)	64.6	14
State Minimum Wage (federal floor is $7.25)	$7.25	1
Average Workers' Compensation Costs (per $100 of payroll)	$1.55	8
Right-to-Work State? (option to join or support a union)	Yes	1
Number of Tax Expenditure Limits (0= least/worst 3=most/best)	0	35

Kentucky

31 Economic Performance Rank

40 Economic Outlook Rank

Economic Performance Rank (1=best 50=worst)

A historical measure based on a state's performance (equally weighted average) in the three important performance variables shown below. These variables are highly influenced by state policy.

Economic Outlook Rank (1=best 50=worst)

A forecast based on a state's standing (equally weighted average) in the 15 important state policy variables shown below. Data reflect state + local rates and revenues and any effect of federal deductibility.

Personal Income Per Capita

Cumulative Growth 1999-2009 **38.6%** **Rank: 29**

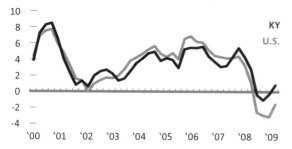

Absolute Domestic Migration

Cumulative 2000-2009 **81,665** **Rank: 15**

(in thousands)

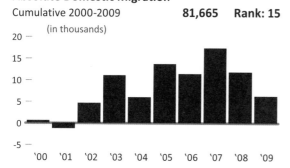

Non-Farm Payroll Employment

Cumulative Growth 1999-2009 **-2.5%** **Rank: 38**

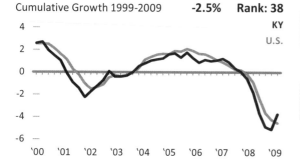

Historical Ranking Comparison	2008	2009	2010
ECONOMIC OUTLOOK RANK	**44**	**36**	**40**

Variable	Data	Rank
Top Marginal Personal Income Tax Rate	8.20%	41
Top Marginal Corporate Income Tax Rate	8.20%	31
Personal Income Tax Progressivity (change in tax liability per $1,000 of income)	$5.38	21
Property Tax Burden (per $1,000 of personal income)	$20.41	7
Sales Tax Burden (per $1,000 of personal income)	$21.11	17
Remaining Tax Burden (per $1,000 of personal income)	$21.53	39
Estate/Inheritance Tax Levied?	Yes	50
Recently Legislated Tax Changes (2009 & 2010, per $1,000 of personal income)	-$3.34	21
Debt Service as a Share of Tax Revenue	11.8%	48
Public Employees Per 10,000 of Population (full-time equivalent)	561.3	29
State Liability System Survey (tort litigation treatment, judicial impartiality, etc.)	54.4	40
State Minimum Wage (federal floor is $7.25)	$7.25	1
Average Workers' Compensation Costs (per $100 of payroll)	$2.29	36
Right-to-Work State? (option to join or support a union)	No	50
Number of Tax Expenditure Limits (0= least/worst 3=most/best)	1	13

Louisiana

27 Economic Performance Rank

15 Economic Outlook Rank

Economic Performance Rank (1=best 50=worst)

A historical measure based on a state's performance (equally weighted average) in the three important performance variables shown below. These variables are highly influenced by state policy.

Economic Outlook Rank (1=best 50=worst)

A forecast based on a state's standing (equally weighted average) in the 15 important state policy variables shown below. Data reflect state + local rates and revenues and any effect of federal deductibility.

Personal Income Per Capita
Cumulative Growth 1999-2009 **63.6%** **Rank: 3**

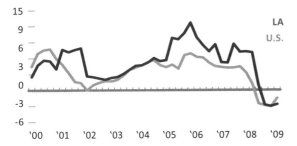

Absolute Domestic Migration
Cumulative 2000-2009 **-307,220** **Rank: 43**

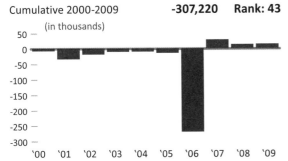

Non-Farm Payroll Employment
Cumulative Growth 1999-2009 **-1.1%** **Rank: 32**

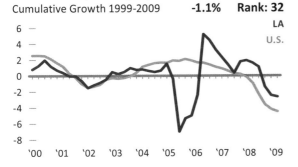

Historical Ranking Comparison	2008	2009	2010
ECONOMIC OUTLOOK RANK	24	18	16

Variable	Data	Rank
Top Marginal Personal Income Tax Rate	3.90%	10
Top Marginal Corporate Income Tax Rate	5.20%	11
Personal Income Tax Progressivity (change in tax liability per $1,000 of income)	$8.35	29
Property Tax Burden (per $1,000 of personal income)	$17.32	6
Sales Tax Burden (per $1,000 of personal income)	$43.37	47
Remaining Tax Burden (per $1,000 of personal income)	$17.34	22
Estate/Inheritance Tax Levied?	No	1
Recently Legislated Tax Changes (2009 & 2010, per $1,000 of personal income)	-$4.72	6
Debt Service as a Share of Tax Revenue	8.8%	35
Public Employees Per 10,000 of Population (full-time equivalent)	616.4	41
State Liability System Survey (tort litigation treatment, judicial impartiality, etc.)	39.6	49
State Minimum Wage (federal floor is $7.25)	$7.25	1
Average Workers' Compensation Costs (per $100 of payroll)	$2.06	26
Right-to-Work State? (option to join or support a union)	Yes	1
Number of Tax Expenditure Limits (0= least/worst 3=most/best)	2	4

Maine

20 Economic Performance Rank

48 Economic Outlook Rank

Economic Performance Rank (1=best 50=worst)

A historical measure based on a state's performance (equally weighted average) in the three important performance variables shown below. These variables are highly influenced by state policy.

Economic Outlook Rank (1=best 50=worst)

A forecast based on a state's standing (equally weighted average) in the 15 important state policy variables shown below. Data reflect state + local rates and revenues and any effect of federal deductibility.

Personal Income Per Capita
Cumulative Growth 1999-2009   **44.4%**   **Rank: 18**

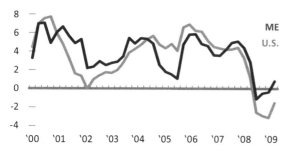

Absolute Domestic Migration
Cumulative 2000-2009   **26,536**   **Rank: 24**

(in thousands)

Non-Farm Payroll Employment
Cumulative Growth 1999-2009   **-0.7%**   **Rank: 29**

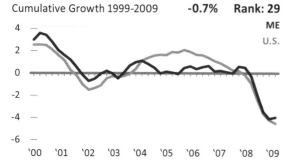

Historical Ranking Comparison	2008	2009	2010
ECONOMIC OUTLOOK RANK	**46**	**47**	**44**

Variable	Data	Rank
Top Marginal Personal Income Tax Rate	8.50%	43
Top Marginal Corporate Income Tax Rate	8.93%	39
Personal Income Tax Progressivity (change in tax liability per $1,000 of income)	$23.31	47
Property Tax Burden (per $1,000 of personal income)	$45.46	45
Sales Tax Burden (per $1,000 of personal income)	$22.35	22
Remaining Tax Burden (per $1,000 of personal income)	$20.22	36
Estate/Inheritance Tax Levied?	Yes	50
Recently Legislated Tax Changes (2009 & 2010, per $1,000 of personal income)	-$0.15	35
Debt Service as a Share of Tax Revenue	6.0%	8
Public Employees Per 10,000 of Population (full-time equivalent)	546.1	24
State Liability System Survey (tort litigation treatment, judicial impartiality, etc.)	65.2	12
State Minimum Wage (federal floor is $7.25)	$7.50	40
Average Workers' Compensation Costs (per $100 of payroll)	$2.52	43
Right-to-Work State? (option to join or support a union)	No	50
Number of Tax Expenditure Limits (0= least/worst 3=most/best)	1	13

Maryland

21 Economic Performance Rank

21 Economic Outlook Rank

Economic Performance Rank (1=best 50=worst)

A historical measure based on a state's performance (equally weighted average) in the three important performance variables shown below. These variables are highly influenced by state policy.

Personal Income Per Capita
Cumulative Growth 1999-2009   **47.3%   Rank: 12**

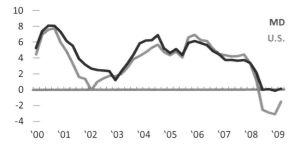

Absolute Domestic Migration
Cumulative 2000-2009   **-96,512   Rank: 41**

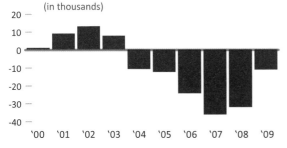

Non-Farm Payroll Employment
Cumulative Growth 1999-2009   **3.2%   Rank: 18**

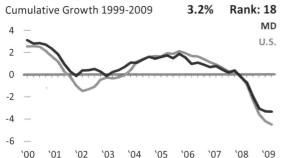

Economic Outlook Rank (1=best 50=worst)

A forecast based on a state's standing (equally weighted average) in the 15 important state policy variables shown below. Data reflect state + local rates and revenues and any effect of federal deductibility.

Historical Ranking Comparison	2008	2009	2010
ECONOMIC OUTLOOK RANK	**28**	**28**	**29**

Variable	Data	Rank
Top Marginal Personal Income Tax Rate	8.55%	44
Top Marginal Corporate Income Tax Rate	8.25%	32
Personal Income Tax Progressivity (change in tax liability per $1,000 of income)	$5.78	22
Property Tax Burden (per $1,000 of personal income)	$24.49	13
Sales Tax Burden (per $1,000 of personal income)	$13.89	8
Remaining Tax Burden (per $1,000 of personal income)	$19.60	32
Estate/Inheritance Tax Levied?	Yes	50
Recently Legislated Tax Changes (2009 & 2010, per $1,000 of personal income)	-$4.06	15
Debt Service as a Share of Tax Revenue	6.0%	7
Public Employees Per 10,000 of Population (full-time equivalent)	528.3	15
State Liability System Survey (tort litigation treatment, judicial impartiality, etc.)	63.2	20
State Minimum Wage (federal floor is $7.25)	$7.25	1
Average Workers' Compensation Costs (per $100 of payroll)	$1.63	9
Right-to-Work State? (option to join or support a union)	No	50
Number of Tax Expenditure Limits (0= least/worst 3=most/best)	0	35

Massachusetts

45
Economic
Performance Rank

24
Economic
Outlook Rank

Economic Performance Rank (1=best 50=worst)
A historical measure based on a state's performance (equally weighted average) in the three important performance variables shown below. These variables are highly influenced by state policy.

Economic Outlook Rank (1=best 50=worst)
A forecast based on a state's standing (equally weighted average) in the 15 important state policy variables shown below. Data reflect state + local rates and revenues and any effect of federal deductibility.

Personal Income Per Capita
Cumulative Growth 1999-2009 **39.2% Rank: 28**

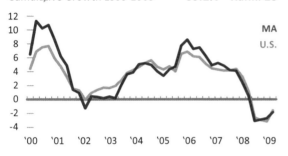

Historical Ranking Comparison	2008	2009	2010
ECONOMIC OUTLOOK RANK	**22**	**26**	**32**

Variable	Data	Rank
Top Marginal Personal Income Tax Rate	5.30%	20
Top Marginal Corporate Income Tax Rate	8.25%	32
Personal Income Tax Progressivity (change in tax liability per $1,000 of income)	$3.11	19
Property Tax Burden (per $1,000 of personal income)	$35.33	35
Sales Tax Burden (per $1,000 of personal income)	$12.41	6
Remaining Tax Burden (per $1,000 of personal income)	$10.70	1
Estate/Inheritance Tax Levied?	Yes	50
Recently Legislated Tax Changes (2009 & 2010, per $1,000 of personal income)	$2.04	41
Debt Service as a Share of Tax Revenue	13.7%	50
Public Employees Per 10,000 of Population (full-time equivalent)	493.4	6
State Liability System Survey (tort litigation treatment, judicial impartiality, etc.)	65.6	9
State Minimum Wage (federal floor is $7.25)	$8.00	43
Average Workers' Compensation Costs (per $100 of payroll)	$1.54	7
Right-to-Work State? (option to join or support a union)	No	50
Number of Tax Expenditure Limits (0= least/worst 3=most/best)	1	13

Absolute Domestic Migration
Cumulative 2000-2009 **-322,183 Rank: 44**
(in thousands)

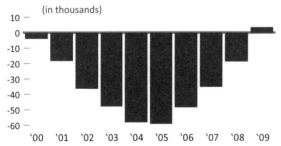

Non-Farm Payroll Employment
Cumulative Growth 1999-2009 **-3.9% Rank: 44**

Michigan

50 Economic Performance Rank

25 Economic Outlook Rank

Economic Performance Rank (1=best 50=worst)
A historical measure based on a state's performance (equally weighted average) in the three important performance variables shown below. These variables are highly influenced by state policy.

Economic Outlook Rank (1=best 50=worst)
A forecast based on a state's standing (equally weighted average) in the 15 important state policy variables shown below. Data reflect state + local rates and revenues and any effect of federal deductibility.

Personal Income Per Capita
Cumulative Growth 1999-2009 **21.2%** **Rank: 50**

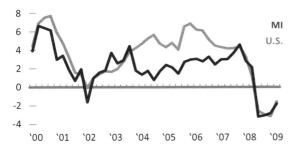

Absolute Domestic Migration
Cumulative 2000-2009 **-555,675** **Rank: 47**

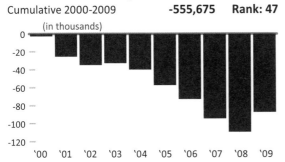

Non-Farm Payroll Employment
Cumulative Growth 1999-2009 **-16.5%** **Rank: 50**

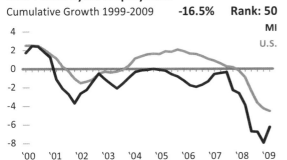

Historical Ranking Comparison	2008	2009	2010
ECONOMIC OUTLOOK RANK	17	34	26

Variable	Data	Rank
Top Marginal Personal Income Tax Rate	6.85%	30
Top Marginal Corporate Income Tax Rate	9.01%	42
Personal Income Tax Progressivity (change in tax liability per $1,000 of income)	$2.09	17
Property Tax Burden (per $1,000 of personal income)	$40.39	40
Sales Tax Burden (per $1,000 of personal income)	$23.52	24
Remaining Tax Burden (per $1,000 of personal income)	$16.42	14
Estate/Inheritance Tax Levied?	No	1
Recently Legislated Tax Changes (2009 & 2010, per $1,000 of personal income)	-$4.54	8
Debt Service as a Share of Tax Revenue	8.8%	34
Public Employees Per 10,000 of Population (full-time equivalent)	475.3	4
State Liability System Survey (tort litigation treatment, judicial impartiality, etc.)	59.5	30
State Minimum Wage (federal floor is $7.25)	$7.40	37
Average Workers' Compensation Costs (per $100 of payroll)	$2.12	28
Right-to-Work State? (option to join or support a union)	No	50
Number of Tax Expenditure Limits (0= least/worst 3=most/best)	2	4

Minnesota

41 Economic Performance Rank

37 Economic Outlook Rank

Economic Performance Rank (1=best 50=worst)

A historical measure based on a state's performance (equally weighted average) in the three important performance variables shown below. These variables are highly influenced by state policy.

Economic Outlook Rank (1=best 50=worst)

A forecast based on a state's standing (equally weighted average) in the 15 important state policy variables shown below. Data reflect state + local rates and revenues and any effect of federal deductibility.

Personal Income Per Capita
Cumulative Growth 1999-2009   **34.6%   Rank: 36**

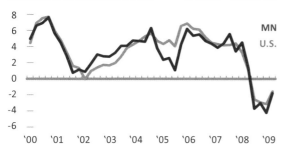

Absolute Domestic Migration
Cumulative 2000-2009   **-51,067   Rank: 37**

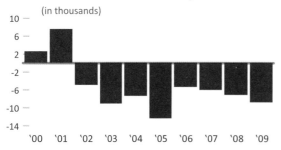

Non-Farm Payroll Employment
Cumulative Growth 1999-2009   **-0.9%   Rank: 30**

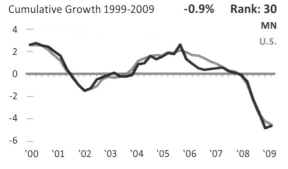

Historical Ranking Comparison	2008	2009	2010
ECONOMIC OUTLOOK RANK	**39**	**40**	**38**

Variable	Data	Rank
Top Marginal Personal Income Tax Rate	7.85%	39
Top Marginal Corporate Income Tax Rate	9.80%	45
Personal Income Tax Progressivity (change in tax liability per $1,000 of income)	$9.17	31
Property Tax Burden (per $1,000 of personal income)	$29.84	22
Sales Tax Burden (per $1,000 of personal income)	$21.00	16
Remaining Tax Burden (per $1,000 of personal income)	$20.53	37
Estate/Inheritance Tax Levied?	Yes	50
Recently Legislated Tax Changes (2009 & 2010, per $1,000 of personal income)	-$3.96	17
Debt Service as a Share of Tax Revenue	7.2%	17
Public Employees Per 10,000 of Population (full-time equivalent)	535.0	18
State Liability System Survey (tort litigation treatment, judicial impartiality, etc.)	65.3	11
State Minimum Wage (federal floor is $7.25)	$7.25	1
Average Workers' Compensation Costs (per $100 of payroll)	$2.27	35
Right-to-Work State? (option to join or support a union)	No	50
Number of Tax Expenditure Limits (0= least/worst 3=most/best)	0	35

Mississippi

39 Economic Performance Rank

19 Economic Outlook Rank

Economic Performance Rank (1=best 50=worst)
A historical measure based on a state's performance (equally weighted average) in the three important performance variables shown below. These variables are highly influenced by state policy.

Economic Outlook Rank (1=best 50=worst)
A forecast based on a state's standing (equally weighted average) in the 15 important state policy variables shown below. Data reflect state + local rates and revenues and any effect of federal deductibility.

Personal Income Per Capita
Cumulative Growth 1999-2009   **45.5%**   **Rank: 16**

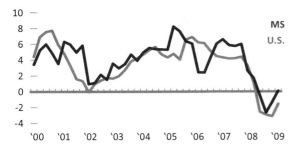

Absolute Domestic Migration
Cumulative 2000-2009   **-36,266**   **Rank: 34**
(in thousands)

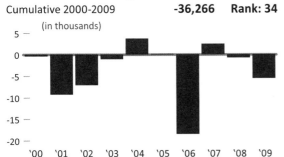

Non-Farm Payroll Employment
Cumulative Growth 1999-2009   **-5.9%**   **Rank: 46**

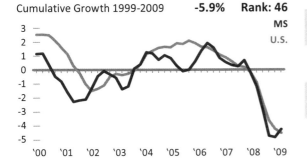

Historical Ranking Comparison	2008	2009	2010
ECONOMIC OUTLOOK RANK	**19**	**19**	**18**

Variable	Data	Rank
Top Marginal Personal Income Tax Rate	5.00%	17
Top Marginal Corporate Income Tax Rate	5.00%	7
Personal Income Tax Progressivity (change in tax liability per $1,000 of income)	$7.53	28
Property Tax Burden (per $1,000 of personal income)	$25.79	16
Sales Tax Burden (per $1,000 of personal income)	$35.16	42
Remaining Tax Burden (per $1,000 of personal income)	$17.69	23
Estate/Inheritance Tax Levied?	No	1
Recently Legislated Tax Changes (2009 & 2010, per $1,000 of personal income)	-$1.46	30
Debt Service as a Share of Tax Revenue	5.9%	6
Public Employees Per 10,000 of Population (full-time equivalent)	655.9	46
State Liability System Survey (tort litigation treatment, judicial impartiality, etc.)	40.0	48
State Minimum Wage (federal floor is $7.25)	$7.25	1
Average Workers' Compensation Costs (per $100 of payroll)	$1.96	20
Right-to-Work State? (option to join or support a union)	Yes	1
Number of Tax Expenditure Limits (0= least/worst 3=most/best)	1	13

Missouri

38 Economic Performance Rank

9 Economic Outlook Rank

Economic Performance Rank (1=best 50=worst)

A historical measure based on a state's performance (equally weighted average) in the three important performance variables shown below. These variables are highly influenced by state policy.

Personal Income Per Capita
Cumulative Growth 1999-2009   **34.2%**   **Rank: 37**

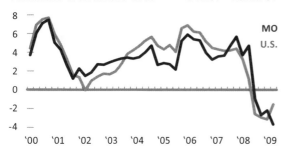

Absolute Domestic Migration
Cumulative 2000-2009   **39,000**   **Rank: 19**

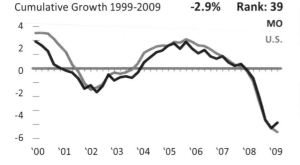

Non-Farm Payroll Employment
Cumulative Growth 1999-2009   **-2.9%**   **Rank: 39**

Economic Outlook Rank (1=best 50=worst)

A forecast based on a state's standing (equally weighted average) in the 15 important state policy variables shown below. Data reflect state + local rates and revenues and any effect of federal deductibility.

Historical Ranking Comparison	2008	2009	2010
ECONOMIC OUTLOOK RANK	**25**	**23**	**15**

Variable	Data	Rank
Top Marginal Personal Income Tax Rate	7.00%	32
Top Marginal Corporate Income Tax Rate	5.81%	15
Personal Income Tax Progressivity (change in tax liability per $1,000 of income)	$0.28	14
Property Tax Burden (per $1,000 of personal income)	$25.59	15
Sales Tax Burden (per $1,000 of personal income)	$23.60	25
Remaining Tax Burden (per $1,000 of personal income)	$15.83	11
Estate/Inheritance Tax Levied?	No	1
Recently Legislated Tax Changes (2009 & 2010, per $1,000 of personal income)	-$4.95	4
Debt Service as a Share of Tax Revenue	9.8%	41
Public Employees Per 10,000 of Population (full-time equivalent)	542.3	22
State Liability System Survey (tort litigation treatment, judicial impartiality, etc.)	56.1	37
State Minimum Wage (federal floor is $7.25)	$7.25	1
Average Workers' Compensation Costs (per $100 of payroll)	$1.90	18
Right-to-Work State? (option to join or support a union)	No	50
Number of Tax Expenditure Limits (0= least/worst 3=most/best)	3	1

Montana

3 Economic Performance Rank

36 Economic Outlook Rank

Economic Performance Rank (1=best 50=worst)
A historical measure based on a state's performance (equally weighted average) in the three important performance variables shown below. These variables are highly influenced by state policy.

Economic Outlook Rank (1=best 50=worst)
A forecast based on a state's standing (equally weighted average) in the 15 important state policy variables shown below. Data reflect state + local rates and revenues and any effect of federal deductibility.

Personal Income Per Capita
Cumulative Growth 1999-2009   **55.7%**   **Rank: 4**

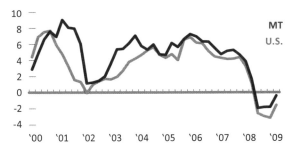

Absolute Domestic Migration
Cumulative 2000-2009   **38,910**   **Rank: 20**

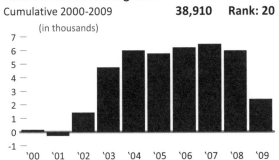

Non-Farm Payroll Employment
Cumulative Growth 1999-2009   **10.2%**   **Rank: 8**

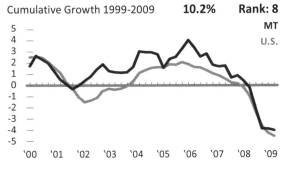

Historical Ranking Comparison	2008	2009	2010
ECONOMIC OUTLOOK RANK	**32**	**30**	**33**

Variable	Data	Rank
Top Marginal Personal Income Tax Rate	6.90%	31
Top Marginal Corporate Income Tax Rate	6.75%	22
Personal Income Tax Progressivity (change in tax liability per $1,000 of income)	$6.09	23
Property Tax Burden (per $1,000 of personal income)	$35.10	34
Sales Tax Burden (per $1,000 of personal income)	$0.00	1
Remaining Tax Burden (per $1,000 of personal income)	$26.61	46
Estate/Inheritance Tax Levied?	No	1
Recently Legislated Tax Changes (2009 & 2010, per $1,000 of personal income)	-$5.19	2
Debt Service as a Share of Tax Revenue	8.2%	28
Public Employees Per 10,000 of Population (full-time equivalent)	580.8	34
State Liability System Survey (tort litigation treatment, judicial impartiality, etc.)	52.4	43
State Minimum Wage (federal floor is $7.25)	$7.35	34
Average Workers' Compensation Costs (per $100 of payroll)	$3.33	50
Right-to-Work State? (option to join or support a union)	No	50
Number of Tax Expenditure Limits (0= least/worst 3=most/best)	1	13

Nebraska

26 Economic Performance Rank

32 Economic Outlook Rank

Economic Performance Rank (1=best 50=worst)

A historical measure based on a state's performance (equally weighted average) in the three important performance variables shown below. These variables are highly influenced by state policy.

Personal Income Per Capita
Cumulative Growth 1999-2009 **41.5%** **Rank: 23**

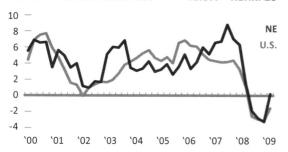

Absolute Domestic Migration
Cumulative 2000-2009 **-39,157** **Rank: 35**

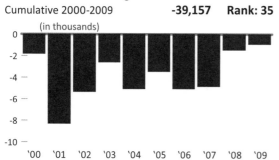

Non-Farm Payroll Employment
Cumulative Growth 1999-2009 **3.6%** **Rank: 16**

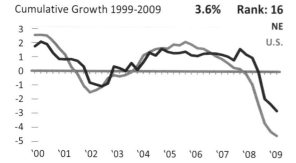

Economic Outlook Rank (1=best 50=worst)

A forecast based on a state's standing (equally weighted average) in the 15 important state policy variables shown below. Data reflect state + local rates and revenues and any effect of federal deductibility.

Historical Ranking Comparison
ECONOMIC OUTLOOK RANK

	2008	2009	2010
ECONOMIC OUTLOOK RANK	34	29	34

Variable	Data	Rank
Top Marginal Personal Income Tax Rate	6.84%	29
Top Marginal Corporate Income Tax Rate	7.81%	29
Personal Income Tax Progressivity (change in tax liability per $1,000 of income)	$16.74	45
Property Tax Burden (per $1,000 of personal income)	$35.40	36
Sales Tax Burden (per $1,000 of personal income)	$26.72	32
Remaining Tax Burden (per $1,000 of personal income)	$16.75	19
Estate/Inheritance Tax Levied?	Yes	50
Recently Legislated Tax Changes (2009 & 2010, per $1,000 of personal income)	-$4.49	9
Debt Service as a Share of Tax Revenue	7.8%	25
Public Employees Per 10,000 of Population (full-time equivalent)	656.6	47
State Liability System Survey (tort litigation treatment, judicial impartiality, etc.)	69.7	4
State Minimum Wage (federal floor is $7.25)	$7.25	1
Average Workers' Compensation Costs (per $100 of payroll)	$1.97	21
Right-to-Work State? (option to join or support a union)	Yes	1
Number of Tax Expenditure Limits (0= least/worst 3=most/best)	0	35

Nevada

18 Economic Performance Rank

17 Economic Outlook Rank

Economic Performance Rank (1=best 50=worst)

A historical measure based on a state's performance (equally weighted average) in the three important performance variables shown below. These variables are highly influenced by state policy.

Economic Outlook Rank (1=best 50=worst)

A forecast based on a state's standing (equally weighted average) in the 15 important state policy variables shown below. Data reflect state + local rates and revenues and any effect of federal deductibility.

Personal Income Per Capita

Cumulative Growth 1999-2009 **23.6%** **Rank: 49**

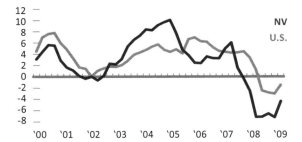

Absolute Domestic Migration

Cumulative 2000-2009 **376,380** **Rank: 6**

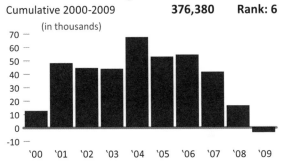

Non-Farm Payroll Employment

Cumulative Growth 1999-2009 **12.4%** **Rank: 4**

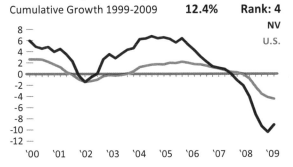

Historical Ranking Comparison	2008	2009	2010
ECONOMIC OUTLOOK RANK	**7**	**7**	**11**

Variable	Data	Rank
Top Marginal Personal Income Tax Rate	0.00%	1
Top Marginal Corporate Income Tax Rate	0.00%	1
Personal Income Tax Progressivity (change in tax liability per $1,000 of income)	$0.00	2
Property Tax Burden (per $1,000 of personal income)	$30.48	25
Sales Tax Burden (per $1,000 of personal income)	$31.97	40
Remaining Tax Burden (per $1,000 of personal income)	$36.51	50
Estate/Inheritance Tax Levied?	No	1
Recently Legislated Tax Changes (2009 & 2010, per $1,000 of personal income)	$3.08	44
Debt Service as a Share of Tax Revenue	9.2%	37
Public Employees Per 10,000 of Population (full-time equivalent)	436.5	1
State Liability System Survey (tort litigation treatment, judicial impartiality, etc.)	59.8	28
State Minimum Wage (federal floor is $7.25)	$8.25	46
Average Workers' Compensation Costs (per $100 of payroll)	$2.13	30
Right-to-Work State? (option to join or support a union)	Yes	1
Number of Tax Expenditure Limits (0= least/worst 3=most/best)	2	4

New Hampshire

29 Economic Performance Rank

28 Economic Outlook Rank

Economic Performance Rank (1=best 50=worst)
A historical measure based on a state's performance (equally weighted average) in the three important performance variables shown below. These variables are highly influenced by state policy.

Economic Outlook Rank (1=best 50=worst)
A forecast based on a state's standing (equally weighted average) in the 15 important state policy variables shown below. Data reflect state + local rates and revenues and any effect of federal deductibility.

Personal Income Per Capita
Cumulative Growth 1999-2009   **34.2%**   **Rank: 38**

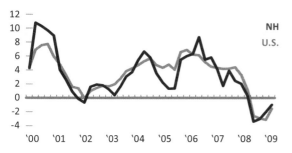

Absolute Domestic Migration
Cumulative 2000-2009   **30,858**   **Rank: 22**

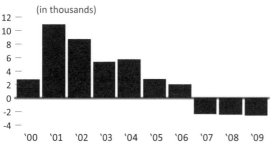

Non-Farm Payroll Employment
Cumulative Growth 1999-2009   **1.7%**   **Rank: 20**

Historical Ranking Comparison	2008	2009	2010
ECONOMIC OUTLOOK RANK	**26**	**37**	**30**

Variable	Data	Rank
Top Marginal Personal Income Tax Rate	0.00%	1
Top Marginal Corporate Income Tax Rate	8.50%	34
Personal Income Tax Progressivity (change in tax liability per $1,000 of income)	$0.00	2
Property Tax Burden (per $1,000 of personal income)	$53.38	50
Sales Tax Burden (per $1,000 of personal income)	$0.00	1
Remaining Tax Burden (per $1,000 of personal income)	$19.80	34
Estate/Inheritance Tax Levied?	No	1
Recently Legislated Tax Changes (2009 & 2010, per $1,000 of personal income)	-$1.36	31
Debt Service as a Share of Tax Revenue	10.0%	43
Public Employees Per 10,000 of Population (full-time equivalent)	541.0	21
State Liability System Survey (tort litigation treatment, judicial impartiality, etc.)	64.2	16
State Minimum Wage (federal floor is $7.25)	$7.25	1
Average Workers' Compensation Costs (per $100 of payroll)	$2.45	41
Right-to-Work State? (option to join or support a union)	No	50
Number of Tax Expenditure Limits (0= least/worst 3=most/best)	0	35

New Jersey

42 Economic Performance Rank

45 Economic Outlook Rank

Economic Performance Rank (1=best 50=worst)

A historical measure based on a state's performance (equally weighted average) in the three important performance variables shown below. These variables are highly influenced by state policy.

Economic Outlook Rank (1=best 50=worst)

A forecast based on a state's standing (equally weighted average) in the 15 important state policy variables shown below. Data reflect state + local rates and revenues and any effect of federal deductibility.

Personal Income Per Capita

Cumulative Growth 1999-2009 **39.4%** **Rank: 27**

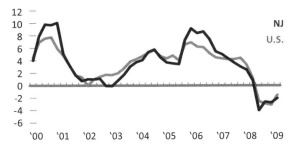

Absolute Domestic Migration

Cumulative 2000-2009 **-464,111** **Rank: 46**

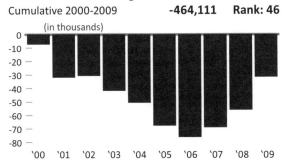

Non-Farm Payroll Employment

Cumulative Growth 1999-2009 **-1.8%** **Rank: 34**

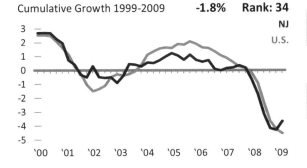

Historical Ranking Comparison	2008	2009	2010
ECONOMIC OUTLOOK RANK	**48**	**46**	**48**

Variable	Data	Rank
Top Marginal Personal Income Tax Rate	8.97%	46
Top Marginal Corporate Income Tax Rate	9.00%	40
Personal Income Tax Progressivity (change in tax liability per $1,000 of income)	$24.81	48
Property Tax Burden (per $1,000 of personal income)	$51.22	49
Sales Tax Burden (per $1,000 of personal income)	$20.11	15
Remaining Tax Burden (per $1,000 of personal income)	$14.50	7
Estate/Inheritance Tax Levied?	Yes	50
Recently Legislated Tax Changes (2009 & 2010, per $1,000 of personal income)	-$1.70	28
Debt Service as a Share of Tax Revenue	6.7%	13
Public Employees Per 10,000 of Population (full-time equivalent)	578.7	33
State Liability System Survey (tort litigation treatment, judicial impartiality, etc.)	57.8	32
State Minimum Wage (federal floor is $7.25)	$7.25	1
Average Workers' Compensation Costs (per $100 of payroll)	$2.53	44
Right-to-Work State? (option to join or support a union)	No	50
Number of Tax Expenditure Limits (0= least/worst 3=most/best)	1	13

New Mexico

5
Economic
Performance Rank

39
Economic
Outlook Rank

Economic Performance Rank (1=best 50=worst)
A historical measure based on a state's performance (equally weighted average) in the three important performance variables shown below. These variables are highly influenced by state policy.

Economic Outlook Rank (1=best 50=worst)
A forecast based on a state's standing (equally weighted average) in the 15 important state policy variables shown below. Data reflect state + local rates and revenues and any effect of federal deductibility.

Personal Income Per Capita
Cumulative Growth 1999-2009   **53.6%**   **Rank: 6**

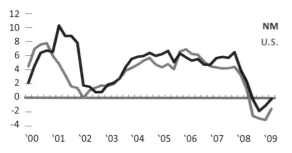

Absolute Domestic Migration
Cumulative 2000-2009   **30,038**   **Rank: 23**

(in thousands)

Non-Farm Payroll Employment
Cumulative Growth 1999-2009   **9.8%**   **Rank: 9**

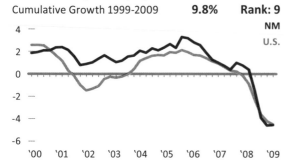

Historical Ranking Comparison	2008	2009	2010
ECONOMIC OUTLOOK RANK	**27**	**25**	**35**

Variable	Data	Rank
Top Marginal Personal Income Tax Rate	4.90%	16
Top Marginal Corporate Income Tax Rate	7.60%	27
Personal Income Tax Progressivity (change in tax liability per $1,000 of income)	$9.84	32
Property Tax Burden (per $1,000 of personal income)	$17.21	5
Sales Tax Burden (per $1,000 of personal income)	$42.35	46
Remaining Tax Burden (per $1,000 of personal income)	$17.79	24
Estate/Inheritance Tax Levied?	No	1
Recently Legislated Tax Changes (2009 & 2010, per $1,000 of personal income)	$1.76	40
Debt Service as a Share of Tax Revenue	7.2%	16
Public Employees Per 10,000 of Population (full-time equivalent)	645.7	45
State Liability System Survey (tort litigation treatment, judicial impartiality, etc.)	53.9	41
State Minimum Wage (federal floor is $7.25)	$7.50	40
Average Workers' Compensation Costs (per $100 of payroll)	$1.91	19
Right-to-Work State? (option to join or support a union)	No	50
Number of Tax Expenditure Limits (0= least/worst 3=most/best)	0	35

New York

40 Economic Performance Rank

50 Economic Outlook Rank

Economic Performance Rank (1=best 50=worst)

A historical measure based on a state's performance (equally weighted average) in the three important performance variables shown below. These variables are highly influenced by state policy.

Economic Outlook Rank (1=best 50=worst)

A forecast based on a state's standing (equally weighted average) in the 15 important state policy variables shown below. Data reflect state + local rates and revenues and any effect of federal deductibility.

Personal Income Per Capita

Cumulative Growth 1999-2009 **42.6%** **Rank: 22**

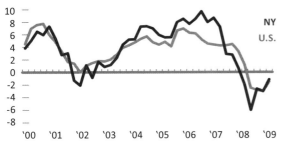

Absolute Domestic Migration

Cumulative 2000-2009 **-1,676,842** **Rank: 50**

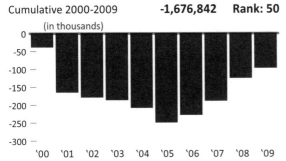

Non-Farm Payroll Employment

Cumulative Growth 1999-2009 **-0.5%** **Rank: 26**

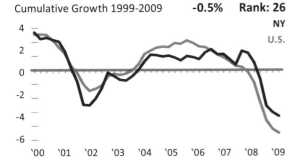

Historical Ranking Comparison	2008	2009	2010
ECONOMIC OUTLOOK RANK	**49**	**50**	**50**

Variable	Data	Rank
Top Marginal Personal Income Tax Rate	12.62%	50
Top Marginal Corporate Income Tax Rate	15.95%	50
Personal Income Tax Progressivity (change in tax liability per $1,000 of income)	$12.71	37
Property Tax Burden (per $1,000 of personal income)	$41.88	43
Sales Tax Burden (per $1,000 of personal income)	$24.69	27
Remaining Tax Burden (per $1,000 of personal income)	$19.65	33
Estate/Inheritance Tax Levied?	Yes	50
Recently Legislated Tax Changes (2009 & 2010, per $1,000 of personal income)	$14.26	50
Debt Service as a Share of Tax Revenue	8.7%	33
Public Employees Per 10,000 of Population (full-time equivalent)	640.8	43
State Liability System Survey (tort litigation treatment, judicial impartiality, etc.)	62.5	23
State Minimum Wage (federal floor is $7.25)	$7.25	1
Average Workers' Compensation Costs (per $100 of payroll)	$2.34	38
Right-to-Work State? (option to join or support a union)	No	50
Number of Tax Expenditure Limits (0= least/worst 3=most/best)	0	35

North Carolina

22 Economic Performance Rank

26 Economic Outlook Rank

Economic Performance Rank (1=best 50=worst)

A historical measure based on a state's performance (equally weighted average) in the three important performance variables shown below. These variables are highly influenced by state policy.

Economic Outlook Rank (1=best 50=worst)

A forecast based on a state's standing (equally weighted average) in the 15 important state policy variables shown below. Data reflect state + local rates and revenues and any effect of federal deductibility.

Personal Income Per Capita

Cumulative Growth 1999-2009   **30.4%**   **Rank: 45**

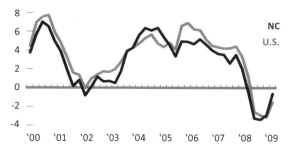

Absolute Domestic Migration

Cumulative 2000-2009   **647,229**   **Rank: 4**

(in thousands)

Non-Farm Payroll Employment

Cumulative Growth 1999-2009   **0.3%**   **Rank: 23**

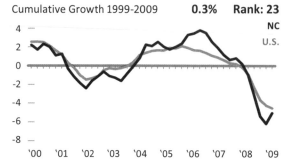

Historical Ranking Comparison	2008	2009	2010
ECONOMIC OUTLOOK RANK	**21**	**21**	**21**

Variable	Data	Rank
Top Marginal Personal Income Tax Rate	7.75%	36
Top Marginal Corporate Income Tax Rate	6.90%	23
Personal Income Tax Progressivity (change in tax liability per $1,000 of income)	$9.87	33
Property Tax Burden (per $1,000 of personal income)	$24.25	12
Sales Tax Burden (per $1,000 of personal income)	$22.26	21
Remaining Tax Burden (per $1,000 of personal income)	$16.83	20
Estate/Inheritance Tax Levied?	Yes	50
Recently Legislated Tax Changes (2009 & 2010, per $1,000 of personal income)	$2.60	43
Debt Service as a Share of Tax Revenue	7.0%	14
Public Employees Per 10,000 of Population (full-time equivalent)	593.6	38
State Liability System Survey (tort litigation treatment, judicial impartiality, etc.)	64.0	17
State Minimum Wage (federal floor is $7.25)	$7.25	1
Average Workers' Compensation Costs (per $100 of payroll)	$2.12	28
Right-to-Work State? (option to join or support a union)	Yes	1
Number of Tax Expenditure Limits (0= least/worst 3=most/best)	1	13

North Dakota

4 Economic Performance Rank

7 Economic Outlook Rank

Economic Performance Rank (1=best 50=worst)
A historical measure based on a state's performance (equally weighted average) in the three important performance variables shown below. These variables are highly influenced by state policy.

Economic Outlook Rank (1=best 50=worst)
A forecast based on a state's standing (equally weighted average) in the 15 important state policy variables shown below. Data reflect state + local rates and revenues and any effect of federal deductibility.

Personal Income Per Capita
Cumulative Growth 1999-2009   **69.5%   Rank: 2**

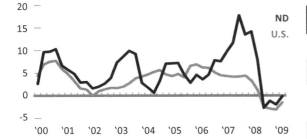

Absolute Domestic Migration
Cumulative 2000-2009   **-18,632   Rank: 31**
(in thousands)

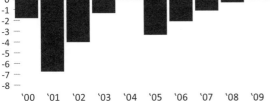

Non-Farm Payroll Employment
Cumulative Growth 1999-2009   **12.5%   Rank: 3**

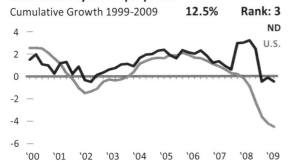

Historical Ranking Comparison	2008	2009	2010
ECONOMIC OUTLOOK RANK	**18**	**13**	**12**

Variable	Data	Rank
Top Marginal Personal Income Tax Rate	4.86%	15
Top Marginal Corporate Income Tax Rate	4.16%	4
Personal Income Tax Progressivity (change in tax liability per $1,000 of income)	$8.91	30
Property Tax Burden (per $1,000 of personal income)	$29.16	20
Sales Tax Burden (per $1,000 of personal income)	$24.52	26
Remaining Tax Burden (per $1,000 of personal income)	$21.32	38
Estate/Inheritance Tax Levied?	No	1
Recently Legislated Tax Changes (2009 & 2010, per $1,000 of personal income)	-$13.84	1
Debt Service as a Share of Tax Revenue	7.7%	23
Public Employees Per 10,000 of Population (full-time equivalent)	644.0	44
State Liability System Survey (tort litigation treatment, judicial impartiality, etc.)	71.1	2
State Minimum Wage (federal floor is $7.25)	$7.25	1
Average Workers' Compensation Costs (per $100 of payroll)	$1.02	1
Right-to-Work State? (option to join or support a union)	Yes	1
Number of Tax Expenditure Limits (0= least/worst 3=most/best)	0	35

Ohio

49 Economic Performance Rank

38 Economic Outlook Rank

Economic Performance Rank (1=best 50=worst)
A historical measure based on a state's performance (equally weighted average) in the three important performance variables shown below. These variables are highly influenced by state policy.

Economic Outlook Rank (1=best 50=worst)
A forecast based on a state's standing (equally weighted average) in the 15 important state policy variables shown below. Data reflect state + local rates and revenues and any effect of federal deductibility.

Personal Income Per Capita
Cumulative Growth 1999-2009 **28.1%** **Rank: 47**

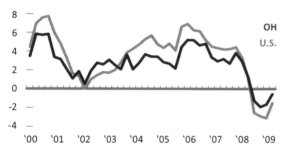

Absolute Domestic Migration
Cumulative 2000-2009 **-388,043** **Rank: 45**

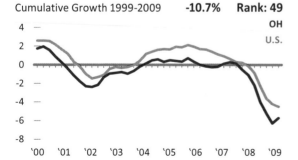

Non-Farm Payroll Employment
Cumulative Growth 1999-2009 **-10.7%** **Rank: 49**

Historical Ranking Comparison	2008	2009	2010
ECONOMIC OUTLOOK RANK	**47**	**45**	**42**

Variable	Data	Rank
Top Marginal Personal Income Tax Rate	7.93%	40
Top Marginal Corporate Income Tax Rate	5.14%	10
Personal Income Tax Progressivity (change in tax liability per $1,000 of income)	$14.53	42
Property Tax Burden (per $1,000 of personal income)	$32.94	30
Sales Tax Burden (per $1,000 of personal income)	$23.12	23
Remaining Tax Burden (per $1,000 of personal income)	$18.52	29
Estate/Inheritance Tax Levied?	Yes	50
Recently Legislated Tax Changes (2009 & 2010, per $1,000 of personal income)	-$0.84	33
Debt Service as a Share of Tax Revenue	7.2%	18
Public Employees Per 10,000 of Population (full-time equivalent)	533.9	17
State Liability System Survey (tort litigation treatment, judicial impartiality, etc.)	59.7	29
State Minimum Wage (federal floor is $7.25)	$7.40	37
Average Workers' Compensation Costs (per $100 of payroll)	$2.24	34
Right-to-Work State? (option to join or support a union)	No	50
Number of Tax Expenditure Limits (0= least/worst 3=most/best)	1	13

Oklahoma

9 Economic Performance Rank

14 Economic Outlook Rank

Economic Performance Rank (1=best 50=worst)
A historical measure based on a state's performance (equally weighted average) in the three important performance variables shown below. These variables are highly influenced by state policy.

Economic Outlook Rank (1=best 50=worst)
A forecast based on a state's standing (equally weighted average) in the 15 important state policy variables shown below. Data reflect state + local rates and revenues and any effect of federal deductibility.

Personal Income Per Capita
Cumulative Growth 1999-2009 **53.7%** **Rank: 5**

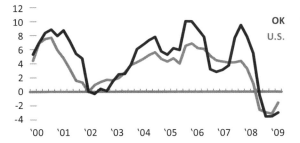

Absolute Domestic Migration
Cumulative 2000-2009 **38,602** **Rank: 21**
(in thousands)

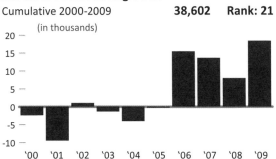

Non-Farm Payroll Employment
Cumulative Growth 1999-2009 **3.3%** **Rank: 17**

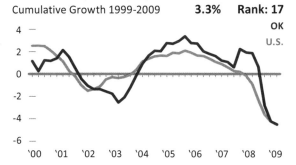

Historical Ranking Comparison	2008	2009	2010
ECONOMIC OUTLOOK RANK	**14**	**15**	**14**

Variable	Data	Rank
Top Marginal Personal Income Tax Rate	5.50%	21
Top Marginal Corporate Income Tax Rate	6.00%	16
Personal Income Tax Progressivity (change in tax liability per $1,000 of income)	$6.94	27
Property Tax Burden (per $1,000 of personal income)	$16.21	3
Sales Tax Burden (per $1,000 of personal income)	$27.72	34
Remaining Tax Burden (per $1,000 of personal income)	$16.92	21
Estate/Inheritance Tax Levied?	No	1
Recently Legislated Tax Changes (2009 & 2010, per $1,000 of personal income)	-$3.32	22
Debt Service as a Share of Tax Revenue	6.3%	9
Public Employees Per 10,000 of Population (full-time equivalent)	590.5	37
State Liability System Survey (tort litigation treatment, judicial impartiality, etc.)	59.0	31
State Minimum Wage (federal floor is $7.25)	$7.25	1
Average Workers' Compensation Costs (per $100 of payroll)	$2.87	47
Right-to-Work State? (option to join or support a union)	Yes	1
Number of Tax Expenditure Limits (0= least/worst 3=most/best)	2	4

Oregon

30 Economic Performance Rank

43 Economic Outlook Rank

Economic Performance Rank (1=best 50=worst)

A historical measure based on a state's performance (equally weighted average) in the three important performance variables shown below. These variables are highly influenced by state policy.

Economic Outlook Rank (1=best 50=worst)

A forecast based on a state's standing (equally weighted average) in the 15 important state policy variables shown below. Data reflect state + local rates and revenues and any effect of federal deductibility.

Personal Income Per Capita
Cumulative Growth 1999-2009 **30.9%** **Rank: 43**

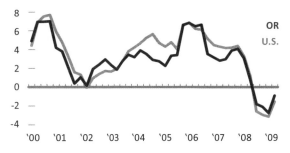

Absolute Domestic Migration
Cumulative 2000-2009 **177,312** **Rank: 11**
(in thousands)

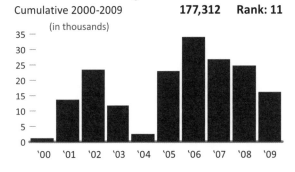

Non-Farm Payroll Employment
Cumulative Growth 1999-2009 **-0.6%** **Rank: 27**

Historical Ranking Comparison	2008	2009	2010
ECONOMIC OUTLOOK RANK	**35**	**39**	**41**

Variable	Data	Rank
Top Marginal Personal Income Tax Rate	11.00%	48
Top Marginal Corporate Income Tax Rate	11.25%	48
Personal Income Tax Progressivity (change in tax liability per $1,000 of income)	$13.37	39
Property Tax Burden (per $1,000 of personal income)	$31.04	28
Sales Tax Burden (per $1,000 of personal income)	$0.00	1
Remaining Tax Burden (per $1,000 of personal income)	$19.91	35
Estate/Inheritance Tax Levied?	Yes	50
Recently Legislated Tax Changes (2009 & 2010, per $1,000 of personal income)	$8.08	48
Debt Service as a Share of Tax Revenue	9.7%	40
Public Employees Per 10,000 of Population (full-time equivalent)	519.4	14
State Liability System Survey (tort litigation treatment, judicial impartiality, etc.)	63.0	21
State Minimum Wage (federal floor is $7.25)	$8.50	49
Average Workers' Compensation Costs (per $100 of payroll)	$1.69	10
Right-to-Work State? (option to join or support a union)	No	50
Number of Tax Expenditure Limits (0= least/worst 3=most/best)	2	4

Pennsylvania

37 Economic Performance Rank

41 Economic Outlook Rank

Economic Performance Rank (1=best 50=worst)
A historical measure based on a state's performance (equally weighted average) in the three important performance variables shown below. These variables are highly influenced by state policy.

Economic Outlook Rank (1=best 50=worst)
A forecast based on a state's standing (equally weighted average) in the 15 important state policy variables shown below. Data reflect state + local rates and revenues and any effect of federal deductibility.

Personal Income Per Capita
Cumulative Growth 1999-2009   **40.5%   Rank: 24**

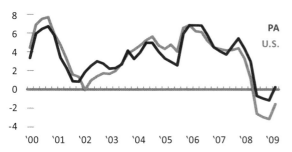

Absolute Domestic Migration
Cumulative 2000-2009   **-52,850   Rank: 39**

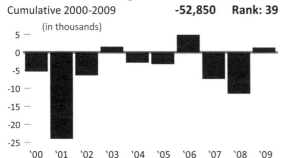

Non-Farm Payroll Employment
Cumulative Growth 1999-2009   **-1.0%   Rank: 31**

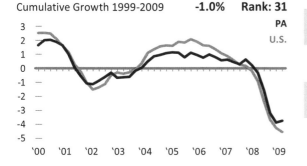

Historical Ranking Comparison	2008	2009	2010
ECONOMIC OUTLOOK RANK	**36**	**42**	**43**

Variable	Data	Rank
Top Marginal Personal Income Tax Rate	7.05%	35
Top Marginal Corporate Income Tax Rate	13.97%	49
Personal Income Tax Progressivity (change in tax liability per $1,000 of income)	$0.00	2
Property Tax Burden (per $1,000 of personal income)	$31.02	27
Sales Tax Burden (per $1,000 of personal income)	$18.35	12
Remaining Tax Burden (per $1,000 of personal income)	$24.02	42
Estate/Inheritance Tax Levied?	Yes	50
Recently Legislated Tax Changes (2009 & 2010, per $1,000 of personal income)	$2.15	42
Debt Service as a Share of Tax Revenue	9.6%	39
Public Employees Per 10,000 of Population (full-time equivalent)	472.7	3
State Liability System Survey (tort litigation treatment, judicial impartiality, etc.)	56.6	33
State Minimum Wage (federal floor is $7.25)	$7.25	1
Average Workers' Compensation Costs (per $100 of payroll)	$2.32	37
Right-to-Work State? (option to join or support a union)	No	50
Number of Tax Expenditure Limits (0= least/worst 3=most/best)	0	35

Rhode Island

35 Economic Performance Rank

42 Economic Outlook Rank

Economic Performance Rank (1=best 50=worst)
A historical measure based on a state's performance (equally weighted average) in the three important performance variables shown below. These variables are highly influenced by state policy.

Economic Outlook Rank (1=best 50=worst)
A forecast based on a state's standing (equally weighted average) in the 15 important state policy variables shown below. Data reflect state + local rates and revenues and any effect of federal deductibility.

Personal Income Per Capita
Cumulative Growth 1999-2009   **47.1%**   **Rank: 13**

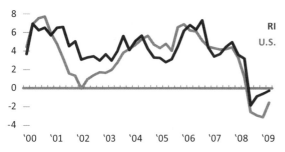

Historical Ranking Comparison	2008	2009	2010
ECONOMIC OUTLOOK RANK	**45**	**48**	**45**

Variable	Data	Rank
Top Marginal Personal Income Tax Rate	5.99%	24
Top Marginal Corporate Income Tax Rate	9.00%	40
Personal Income Tax Progressivity (change in tax liability per $1,000 of income)	$26.36	49
Property Tax Burden (per $1,000 of personal income)	$47.79	46
Sales Tax Burden (per $1,000 of personal income)	$19.49	13
Remaining Tax Burden (per $1,000 of personal income)	$16.60	17
Estate/Inheritance Tax Levied?	Yes	50
Recently Legislated Tax Changes (2009 & 2010, per $1,000 of personal income)	-$3.13	23
Debt Service as a Share of Tax Revenue	10.5%	45
Public Employees Per 10,000 of Population (full-time equivalent)	497.0	8
State Liability System Survey (tort litigation treatment, judicial impartiality, etc.)	55.2	38
State Minimum Wage (federal floor is $7.25)	$7.40	37
Average Workers' Compensation Costs (per $100 of payroll)	$2.02	23
Right-to-Work State? (option to join or support a union)	No	50
Number of Tax Expenditure Limits (0= least/worst 3=most/best)	1	13

Absolute Domestic Migration
Cumulative 2000-2009   **-45,174**   **Rank: 36**

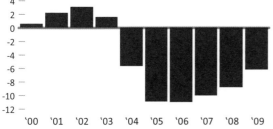

Non-Farm Payroll Employment
Cumulative Growth 1999-2009   **-3.8%**   **Rank: 43**

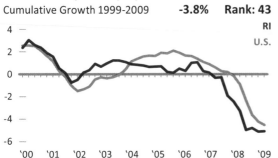

South Carolina

25 Economic Performance Rank

22 Economic Outlook Rank

Economic Performance Rank (1=best 50=worst)
A historical measure based on a state's performance (equally weighted average) in the three important performance variables shown below. These variables are highly influenced by state policy.

Economic Outlook Rank (1=best 50=worst)
A forecast based on a state's standing (equally weighted average) in the 15 important state policy variables shown below. Data reflect state + local rates and revenues and any effect of federal deductibility.

Personal Income Per Capita
Cumulative Growth 1999-2009   **35.8%**   **Rank: 31**

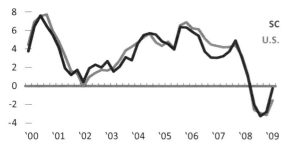

Absolute Domestic Migration
Cumulative 2000-2009   **309,032**   **Rank: 7**
(in thousands)

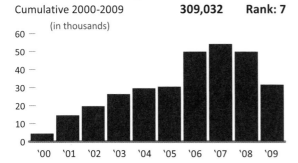

Non-Farm Payroll Employment
Cumulative Growth 1999-2009   **-2.2%**   **Rank: 36**

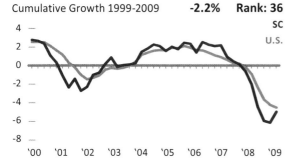

Historical Ranking Comparison	2008	2009	2010
ECONOMIC OUTLOOK RANK	**20**	**20**	**31**

Variable	Data	Rank
Top Marginal Personal Income Tax Rate	7.00%	33
Top Marginal Corporate Income Tax Rate	5.00%	7
Personal Income Tax Progressivity (change in tax liability per $1,000 of income)	$6.21	24
Property Tax Burden (per $1,000 of personal income)	$29.44	21
Sales Tax Burden (per $1,000 of personal income)	$21.73	19
Remaining Tax Burden (per $1,000 of personal income)	$16.61	18
Estate/Inheritance Tax Levied?	No	1
Recently Legislated Tax Changes (2009 & 2010, per $1,000 of personal income)	-$3.68	20
Debt Service as a Share of Tax Revenue	12.1%	49
Public Employees Per 10,000 of Population (full-time equivalent)	557.9	28
State Liability System Survey (tort litigation treatment, judicial impartiality, etc.)	55.1	39
State Minimum Wage (federal floor is $7.25)	$7.25	1
Average Workers' Compensation Costs (per $100 of payroll)	$2.38	39
Right-to-Work State? (option to join or support a union)	Yes	1
Number of Tax Expenditure Limits (0= least/worst 3=most/best)	1	13

South Dakota

11 Economic Performance Rank

2 Economic Outlook Rank

Economic Performance Rank (1=best 50=worst)

A historical measure based on a state's performance (equally weighted average) in the three important performance variables shown below. These variables are highly influenced by state policy.

Economic Outlook Rank (1=best 50=worst)

A forecast based on a state's standing (equally weighted average) in the 15 important state policy variables shown below. Data reflect state + local rates and revenues and any effect of federal deductibility.

Personal Income Per Capita

Cumulative Growth 1999-2009   **49.9%**   **Rank: 10**

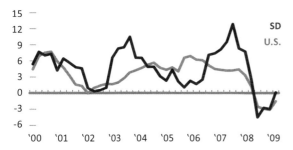

Absolute Domestic Migration

Cumulative 2000-2009   **6,361**   **Rank: 27**

(in thousands)

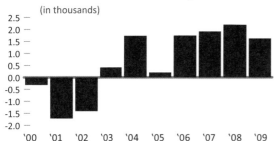

Non-Farm Payroll Employment

Cumulative Growth 1999-2009   **7.3%**   **Rank: 12**

Historical Ranking Comparison	2008	2009	2010
ECONOMIC OUTLOOK RANK	**2**	**5**	**4**

Variable	Data	Rank
Top Marginal Personal Income Tax Rate	0.00%	1
Top Marginal Corporate Income Tax Rate	0.00%	1
Personal Income Tax Progressivity (change in tax liability per $1,000 of income)	$0.00	2
Property Tax Burden (per $1,000 of personal income)	$27.88	18
Sales Tax Burden (per $1,000 of personal income)	$32.57	41
Remaining Tax Burden (per $1,000 of personal income)	$18.11	26
Estate/Inheritance Tax Levied?	No	1
Recently Legislated Tax Changes (2009 & 2010, per $1,000 of personal income)	-$4.27	12
Debt Service as a Share of Tax Revenue	8.3%	29
Public Employees Per 10,000 of Population (full-time equivalent)	589.7	36
State Liability System Survey (tort litigation treatment, judicial impartiality, etc.)	65.6	9
State Minimum Wage (federal floor is $7.25)	$7.25	1
Average Workers' Compensation Costs (per $100 of payroll)	$2.02	23
Right-to-Work State? (option to join or support a union)	Yes	1
Number of Tax Expenditure Limits (0= least/worst 3=most/best)	1	13

Tennessee

36 Economic Performance Rank

8 Economic Outlook Rank

Economic Performance Rank (1=best 50=worst)
A historical measure based on a state's performance (equally weighted average) in the three important performance variables shown below. These variables are highly influenced by state policy.

Personal Income Per Capita
Cumulative Growth 1999-2009   **32.7%   Rank: 41**

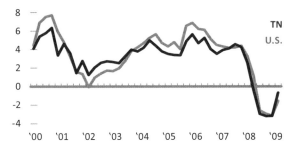

Absolute Domestic Migration
Cumulative 2000-2009   **269,273   Rank: 8**
(in thousands)

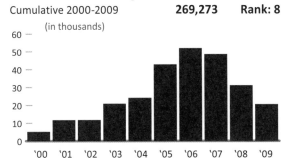

Non-Farm Payroll Employment
Cumulative Growth 1999-2009   **-4.3%   Rank: 45**

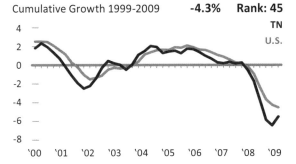

Economic Outlook Rank (1=best 50=worst)
A forecast based on a state's standing (equally weighted average) in the 15 important state policy variables shown below. Data reflect state + local rates and revenues and any effect of federal deductibility.

Historical Ranking Comparison	2008	2009	2010
ECONOMIC OUTLOOK RANK	**3**	**9**	**10**

Variable	Data	Rank
Top Marginal Personal Income Tax Rate	0.00%	1
Top Marginal Corporate Income Tax Rate	6.50%	20
Personal Income Tax Progressivity (change in tax liability per $1,000 of income)	$0.00	2
Property Tax Burden (per $1,000 of personal income)	$21.55	8
Sales Tax Burden (per $1,000 of personal income)	$40.59	44
Remaining Tax Burden (per $1,000 of personal income)	$16.55	16
Estate/Inheritance Tax Levied?	Yes	50
Recently Legislated Tax Changes (2009 & 2010, per $1,000 of personal income)	-$2.71	24
Debt Service as a Share of Tax Revenue	7.6%	22
Public Employees Per 10,000 of Population (full-time equivalent)	516.9	12
State Liability System Survey (tort litigation treatment, judicial impartiality, etc.)	63.7	19
State Minimum Wage (federal floor is $7.25)	$7.25	1
Average Workers' Compensation Costs (per $100 of payroll)	$2.19	31
Right-to-Work State? (option to join or support a union)	Yes	1
Number of Tax Expenditure Limits (0= least/worst 3=most/best)	1	13

Texas

2 Economic Performance Rank

18 Economic Outlook Rank

Economic Performance Rank (1=best 50=worst)
A historical measure based on a state's performance (equally weighted average) in the three important performance variables shown below. These variables are highly influenced by state policy.

Economic Outlook Rank (1=best 50=worst)
A forecast based on a state's standing (equally weighted average) in the 15 important state policy variables shown below. Data reflect state + local rates and revenues and any effect of federal deductibility.

Personal Income Per Capita
Cumulative Growth 1999-2009   **42.8%   Rank: 21**

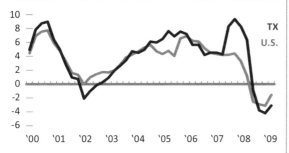

Absolute Domestic Migration
Cumulative 2000-2009   **867,273   Rank: 2**
(in thousands)

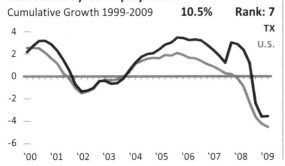

Non-Farm Payroll Employment
Cumulative Growth 1999-2009   **10.5%   Rank: 7**

Historical Ranking Comparison	2008	2009	2010
ECONOMIC OUTLOOK RANK	**13**	**10**	**19**

Variable	Data	Rank
Top Marginal Personal Income Tax Rate	0.00%	1
Top Marginal Corporate Income Tax Rate	5.56%	14
Personal Income Tax Progressivity (change in tax liability per $1,000 of income)	$0.00	2
Property Tax Burden (per $1,000 of personal income)	$36.06	37
Sales Tax Burden (per $1,000 of personal income)	$29.11	37
Remaining Tax Burden (per $1,000 of personal income)	$18.47	28
Estate/Inheritance Tax Levied?	No	1
Recently Legislated Tax Changes (2009 & 2010, per $1,000 of personal income)	-$4.57	7
Debt Service as a Share of Tax Revenue	11.1%	47
Public Employees Per 10,000 of Population (full-time equivalent)	570.4	32
State Liability System Survey (tort litigation treatment, judicial impartiality, etc.)	56.3	36
State Minimum Wage (federal floor is $7.25)	$7.25	1
Average Workers' Compensation Costs (per $100 of payroll)	$2.38	39
Right-to-Work State? (option to join or support a union)	Yes	1
Number of Tax Expenditure Limits (0= least/worst 3=most/best)	1	13

Utah

14 Economic Performance Rank

1 Economic Outlook Rank

Economic Performance Rank (1=best 50=worst)

A historical measure based on a state's performance (equally weighted average) in the three important performance variables shown below. These variables are highly influenced by state policy.

Economic Outlook Rank (1=best 50=worst)

A forecast based on a state's standing (equally weighted average) in the 15 important state policy variables shown below. Data reflect state + local rates and revenues and any effect of federal deductibility.

Personal Income Per Capita

Cumulative Growth 1999-2009   **35.2%   Rank: 32**

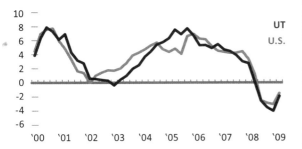

Absolute Domestic Migration

Cumulative 2000-2009   **55,799   Rank: 17**

(in thousands)

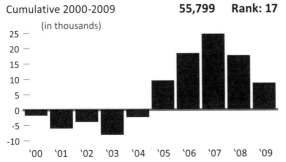

Non-Farm Payroll Employment

Cumulative Growth 1999-2009   **11.8%   Rank: 5**

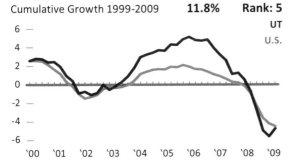

Historical Ranking Comparison	2008	2009	2010
ECONOMIC OUTLOOK RANK	**1**	**1**	**1**

Variable	Data	Rank
Top Marginal Personal Income Tax Rate	5.00%	17
Top Marginal Corporate Income Tax Rate	5.00%	7
Personal Income Tax Progressivity (change in tax liability per $1,000 of income)	$0.00	2
Property Tax Burden (per $1,000 of personal income)	$25.31	14
Sales Tax Burden (per $1,000 of personal income)	$29.82	38
Remaining Tax Burden (per $1,000 of personal income)	$16.47	15
Estate/Inheritance Tax Levied?	No	1
Recently Legislated Tax Changes (2009 & 2010, per $1,000 of personal income)	-$4.12	13
Debt Service as a Share of Tax Revenue	7.3%	19
Public Employees Per 10,000 of Population (full-time equivalent)	503.0	10
State Liability System Survey (tort litigation treatment, judicial impartiality, etc.)	67.8	7
State Minimum Wage (federal floor is $7.25)	$7.25	1
Average Workers' Compensation Costs (per $100 of payroll)	$1.46	6
Right-to-Work State? (option to join or support a union)	Yes	1
Number of Tax Expenditure Limits (0= least/worst 3=most/best)	1	13

Vermont

19 Economic Performance Rank

49 Economic Outlook Rank

Economic Performance Rank (1=best 50=worst)
A historical measure based on a state's performance (equally weighted average) in the three important performance variables shown below. These variables are highly influenced by state policy.

Economic Outlook Rank (1=best 50=worst)
A forecast based on a state's standing (equally weighted average) in the 15 important state policy variables shown below. Data reflect state + local rates and revenues and any effect of federal deductibility.

Personal Income Per Capita
Cumulative Growth 1999-2009   **46.8%   Rank: 14**

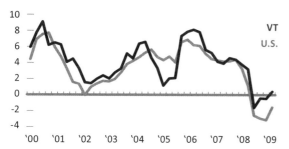

Historical Ranking Comparison	2008	2009	2010
ECONOMIC OUTLOOK RANK	**50**	**49**	**49**

Variable	Data	Rank
Top Marginal Personal Income Tax Rate	8.95%	45
Top Marginal Corporate Income Tax Rate	8.50%	34
Personal Income Tax Progressivity (change in tax liability per $1,000 of income)	$21.26	46
Property Tax Burden (per $1,000 of personal income)	$48.92	47
Sales Tax Burden (per $1,000 of personal income)	$14.31	9
Remaining Tax Burden (per $1,000 of personal income)	$29.15	47
Estate/Inheritance Tax Levied?	Yes	50
Recently Legislated Tax Changes (2009 & 2010, per $1,000 of personal income)	-$0.78	34
Debt Service as a Share of Tax Revenue	7.5%	20
Public Employees Per 10,000 of Population (full-time equivalent)	618.4	42
State Liability System Survey (tort litigation treatment, judicial impartiality, etc.)	61.6	25
State Minimum Wage (federal floor is $7.25)	$8.15	45
Average Workers' Compensation Costs (per $100 of payroll)	$2.22	33
Right-to-Work State? (option to join or support a union)	No	50
Number of Tax Expenditure Limits (0= least/worst 3=most/best)	0	35

Absolute Domestic Migration
Cumulative 2000-2009   **-2,990   Rank: 28**

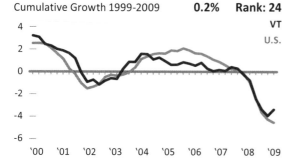

Non-Farm Payroll Employment
Cumulative Growth 1999-2009   **0.2%   Rank: 24**

Virginia

6 Economic Performance Rank

3 Economic Outlook Rank

Economic Performance Rank (1=best 50=worst)
A historical measure based on a state's performance (equally weighted average) in the three important performance variables shown below. These variables are highly influenced by state policy.

Economic Outlook Rank (1=best 50=worst)
A forecast based on a state's standing (equally weighted average) in the 15 important state policy variables shown below. Data reflect state + local rates and revenues and any effect of federal deductibility.

Personal Income Per Capita
Cumulative Growth 1999-2009 **46.2%** **Rank: 15**

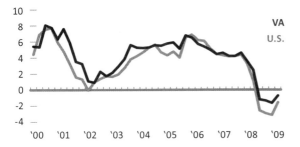

Absolute Domestic Migration
Cumulative 2000-2009 **175,430** **Rank: 12**
(in thousands)

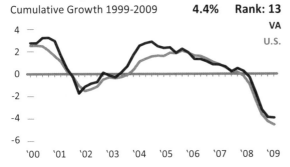

Non-Farm Payroll Employment
Cumulative Growth 1999-2009 **4.4%** **Rank: 13**

Historical Ranking Comparison	2008	2009	2010
ECONOMIC OUTLOOK RANK	**5**	**4**	**8**

Variable	Data	Rank
Top Marginal Personal Income Tax Rate	5.75%	22
Top Marginal Corporate Income Tax Rate	6.00%	16
Personal Income Tax Progressivity (change in tax liability per $1,000 of income)	$6.45	25
Property Tax Burden (per $1,000 of personal income)	$30.78	26
Sales Tax Burden (per $1,000 of personal income)	$13.79	7
Remaining Tax Burden (per $1,000 of personal income)	$18.68	31
Estate/Inheritance Tax Levied?	No	1
Recently Legislated Tax Changes (2009 & 2010, per $1,000 of personal income)	-$4.46	10
Debt Service as a Share of Tax Revenue	6.4%	11
Public Employees Per 10,000 of Population (full-time equivalent)	564.1	31
State Liability System Survey (tort litigation treatment, judicial impartiality, etc.)	68.1	6
State Minimum Wage (federal floor is $7.25)	$7.25	1
Average Workers' Compensation Costs (per $100 of payroll)	$1.39	4
Right-to-Work State? (option to join or support a union)	Yes	1
Number of Tax Expenditure Limits (0= least/worst 3=most/best)	0	35

Washington

13 Economic Performance Rank

33 Economic Outlook Rank

Economic Performance Rank (1=best 50=worst)
A historical measure based on a state's performance (equally weighted average) in the three important performance variables shown below. These variables are highly influenced by state policy.

Economic Outlook Rank (1=best 50=worst)
A forecast based on a state's standing (equally weighted average) in the 15 important state policy variables shown below. Data reflect state + local rates and revenues and any effect of federal deductibility.

Personal Income Per Capita
Cumulative Growth 1999-2009   **36.2%**   **Rank: 30**

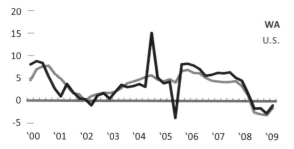

Historical Ranking Comparison	2008	2009	2010
ECONOMIC OUTLOOK RANK	**30**	**22**	**24**

Variable	Data	Rank
Top Marginal Personal Income Tax Rate	0.00%	1
Top Marginal Corporate Income Tax Rate	5.22%	12
Personal Income Tax Progressivity (change in tax liability per $1,000 of income)	$0.00	2
Property Tax Burden (per $1,000 of personal income)	$27.71	17
Sales Tax Burden (per $1,000 of personal income)	$48.73	50
Remaining Tax Burden (per $1,000 of personal income)	$24.70	44
Estate/Inheritance Tax Levied?	Yes	50
Recently Legislated Tax Changes (2009 & 2010, per $1,000 of personal income)	-$0.07	36
Debt Service as a Share of Tax Revenue	10.1%	44
Public Employees Per 10,000 of Population (full-time equivalent)	544.7	23
State Liability System Survey (tort litigation treatment, judicial impartiality, etc.)	61.6	25
State Minimum Wage (federal floor is $7.25)	$8.67	50
Average Workers' Compensation Costs (per $100 of payroll)	$2.04	25
Right-to-Work State? (option to join or support a union)	No	50
Number of Tax Expenditure Limits (0= least/worst 3=most/best)	3	1

Absolute Domestic Migration
Cumulative 2000-2009   **234,730**   **Rank: 9**
(in thousands)

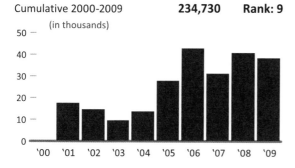

Non-Farm Payroll Employment
Cumulative Growth 1999-2009   **4.0%**   **Rank: 14**

West Virginia

16 Economic Performance Rank

31 Economic Outlook Rank

Economic Performance Rank (1=best 50=worst)
A historical measure based on a state's performance (equally weighted average) in the three important performance variables shown below. These variables are highly influenced by state policy.

Personal Income Per Capita
Cumulative Growth 1999-2009 **50.6%** **Rank: 8**

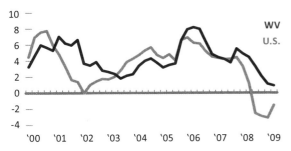

Absolute Domestic Migration
Cumulative 2000-2009 **16,590** **Rank: 26**
(in thousands)

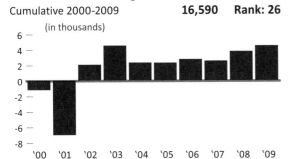

Non-Farm Payroll Employment
Cumulative Growth 1999-2009 **0.8%** **Rank: 21**

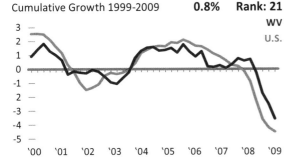

Economic Outlook Rank (1=best 50=worst)
A forecast based on a state's standing (equally weighted average) in the 15 important state policy variables shown below. Data reflect state + local rates and revenues and any effect of federal deductibility.

Historical Ranking Comparison	2008	2009	2010
ECONOMIC OUTLOOK RANK	**38**	**33**	**27**

Variable	Data	Rank
Top Marginal Personal Income Tax Rate	6.50%	27
Top Marginal Corporate Income Tax Rate	8.50%	34
Personal Income Tax Progressivity (change in tax liability per $1,000 of income)	$15.53	43
Property Tax Burden (per $1,000 of personal income)	$22.26	9
Sales Tax Burden (per $1,000 of personal income)	$19.96	14
Remaining Tax Burden (per $1,000 of personal income)	$29.97	48
Estate/Inheritance Tax Levied?	No	1
Recently Legislated Tax Changes (2009 & 2010, per $1,000 of personal income)	-$5.06	3
Debt Service as a Share of Tax Revenue	6.6%	12
Public Employees Per 10,000 of Population (full-time equivalent)	557.0	27
State Liability System Survey (tort litigation treatment, judicial impartiality, etc.)	35.1	50
State Minimum Wage (federal floor is $7.25)	$7.25	1
Average Workers' Compensation Costs (per $100 of payroll)	$1.84	16
Right-to-Work State? (option to join or support a union)	No	50
Number of Tax Expenditure Limits (0= least/worst 3=most/best)	0	35

Wisconsin

44 Economic Performance Rank

30 Economic Outlook Rank

Economic Performance Rank (1=best 50=worst)
A historical measure based on a state's performance (equally weighted average) in the three important performance variables shown below. These variables are highly influenced by state policy.

Economic Outlook Rank (1=best 50=worst)
A forecast based on a state's standing (equally weighted average) in the 15 important state policy variables shown below. Data reflect state + local rates and revenues and any effect of federal deductibility.

Personal Income Per Capita
Cumulative Growth 1999-2009 **33.2%** **Rank: 40**

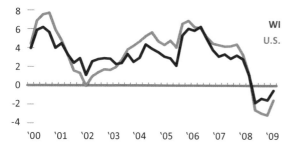

Absolute Domestic Migration
Cumulative 2000-2009 **-18,365** **Rank: 30**

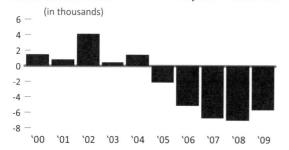

Non-Farm Payroll Employment
Cumulative Growth 1999-2009 **-3.4%** **Rank: 41**

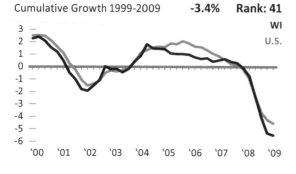

Historical Ranking Comparison	2008	2009	2010
ECONOMIC OUTLOOK RANK	**33**	**27**	**23**

Variable	Data	Rank
Top Marginal Personal Income Tax Rate	7.75%	36
Top Marginal Corporate Income Tax Rate	7.90%	30
Personal Income Tax Progressivity (change in tax liability per $1,000 of income)	$3.67	20
Property Tax Burden (per $1,000 of personal income)	$41.96	44
Sales Tax Burden (per $1,000 of personal income)	$21.70	18
Remaining Tax Burden (per $1,000 of personal income)	$16.38	13
Estate/Inheritance Tax Levied?	No	1
Recently Legislated Tax Changes (2009 & 2010, per $1,000 of personal income)	$4.16	47
Debt Service as a Share of Tax Revenue	7.7%	24
Public Employees Per 10,000 of Population (full-time equivalent)	517.6	13
State Liability System Survey (tort litigation treatment, judicial impartiality, etc.)	62.8	22
State Minimum Wage (federal floor is $7.25)	$7.25	1
Average Workers' Compensation Costs (per $100 of payroll)	$2.21	32
Right-to-Work State? (option to join or support a union)	No	50
Number of Tax Expenditure Limits (0= least/worst 3=most/best)	1	13

Wyoming

1 Economic Performance Rank

4 Economic Outlook Rank

Economic Performance Rank (1=best 50=worst)
A historical measure based on a state's performance (equally weighted average) in the three important performance variables shown below. These variables are highly influenced by state policy.

Economic Outlook Rank (1=best 50=worst)
A forecast based on a state's standing (equally weighted average) in the 15 important state policy variables shown below. Data reflect state + local rates and revenues and any effect of federal deductibility.

Personal Income Per Capita
Cumulative Growth 1999-2009 **70.7%** **Rank: 1**

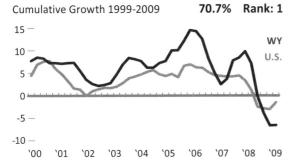

Historical Ranking Comparison	2008	2009	2010
ECONOMIC OUTLOOK RANK	**4**	**6**	**6**

Variable	Data	Rank
Top Marginal Personal Income Tax Rate	0.00%	1
Top Marginal Corporate Income Tax Rate	0.00%	1
Personal Income Tax Progressivity (change in tax liability per $1,000 of income)	$0.00	2
Property Tax Burden (per $1,000 of personal income)	$49.20	48
Sales Tax Burden (per $1,000 of personal income)	$47.50	48
Remaining Tax Burden (per $1,000 of personal income)	$12.61	4
Estate/Inheritance Tax Levied?	No	1
Recently Legislated Tax Changes (2009 & 2010, per $1,000 of personal income)	-$4.34	11
Debt Service as a Share of Tax Revenue	2.8%	1
Public Employees Per 10,000 of Population (full-time equivalent)	948.9	50
State Liability System Survey (tort litigation treatment, judicial impartiality, etc.)	64.5	15
State Minimum Wage (federal floor is $7.25)	$7.25	1
Average Workers' Compensation Costs (per $100 of payroll)	$1.79	14
Right-to-Work State? (option to join or support a union)	Yes	1
Number of Tax Expenditure Limits (0= least/worst 3=most/best)	0	35

Absolute Domestic Migration
Cumulative 2000-2009 **22,235** **Rank: 25**
(in thousands)

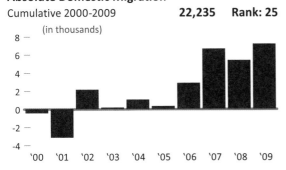

Non-Farm Payroll Employment
Cumulative Growth 1999-2009 **19.4%** **Rank: 1**

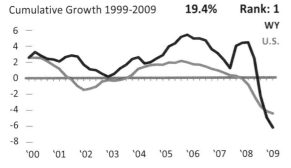

Appendix

2011 ALEC-Laffer State Economic Competitiveness Index:

Economic Outlook Methodology

E arlier in this book, we introduced 15 policy variables that have a proven impact on the migration of capital—both investment and human—into and out of states. The end result of an equally weighted combination of these variables is the 2011 ALEC-Laffer Economic Outlook rankings of the states. Each of these factors is influenced directly by state lawmakers through the legislative process. The 15 factors and a basic description of their purposes, sourcing, and subsequent calculation methodologies are as follows:

HIGHEST MARGINAL PERSONAL INCOME TAX RATE
This ranking includes local taxes, if any, and any impact of federal deductibility, if allowed. A state's largest city was used as a proxy for local tax rates. Data was drawn from: CCH Tax Research Network, Tax Analysts, and Tax Administrators.

HIGHEST MARGINAL CORPORATE INCOME TAX RATE
This variable includes local taxes, if any, and includes the effect of federal deductibility, if allowed. A state's largest city was used as a proxy for local tax rates. In the case of gross receipts or business franchise taxes, an effective tax rate was approximated, when possible, using NIPA profits and gross domestic product data. Data was drawn from: CCH Tax Research Network, Tax Analysts, Tax Administrators, and the Bureau of Economic Analysis.

PERSONAL INCOME TAX PROGRESSIVITY
This variable was measured as the difference between the average tax liability per $1,000 at incomes of $150,000 and $50,000. The tax liabilities were measured using a combination of effective tax rates, exemptions, and deductions at both state and federal levels, which are calculations from Laffer Associates.

PROPERTY TAX BURDEN
This variable was calculated by taking tax revenues from property taxes per $1,000 of personal income. We have used U.S. Census Bureau data, for which the most recent year available is 2008. This data was released in July 2010.

SALES TAX BURDEN
This variable was calculated by taking tax revenues from sales taxes per $1,000 of personal income. Sales taxes taken into consideration include the general sales tax and specific sales taxes. We have used U.S. Census Bureau Data, for which the most recent year available is 2008. This data was released in July 2010.

REMAINING TAX BURDEN
This variable was calculated by taking tax revenues from all taxes—excluding personal income,

corporate income (including corporate license), property, sales, and severance per $1,000 of personal income. We used U.S. Census Bureau Data, for which the most recent year available is 2008. Data was released in July 2010.

ESTATE OR INHERITANCE TAX (YES OR NO)

This variable assesses if a state levies an estate or inheritance tax. We chose to score states based on either a "yes" for the presence of a state-level estate or inheritance tax, or a "no" for the lack thereof. Data was drawn from: American College of Trust and Estate Counsel, "2009 Death Tax Chart: Update January 2010."

RECENTLY LEGISLATED TAX CHANGES

This variable calculates each state's relative change in tax burden over a two year period, (in this case, 2009 and 2010), using static revenue estimates of legislated tax changes per $1000 of personal income. This time frame ensures that tax changes will impact a state's ranking long enough to overcome any lags in the tax revenue data. Laffer Associates calculations used raw data from Tax Analysts and other sources.

DEBT SERVICE AS A SHARE OF TAX REVENUE

Interest paid on debt as a percentage of total tax revenue. This information comes from U.S. Census Bureau data.

PUBLIC EMPLOYEES PER 10,000 RESIDENTS

This variable shows the full-time Equivalent Public Employment per 10,000 of Population. This information comes from U.S. Census Bureau data.

QUALITY OF STATE LEGAL SYSTEM

This variable ranks tort systems by state. Information comes from the 2010 U.S. Chamber of Commerce State Liability Systems Ranking.

STATE MINIMUM WAGE

Minimum wage enforced on a state-by-state basis. If a state does not have a minimum wage, we use the federal minimum wage floor. This information comes from the U.S. Department of Labor, as of December 2010.

WORKERS' COMPENSATION COSTS

This variable highlights the 2010 Workers' Compensation Index Rate (cost per $100 of payroll). Note: This survey is conducted by the Information Management Division, Department of Consumer & Business Services.

RIGHT-TO-WORK STATE (YES OR NO)

This variable assesses whether or not a state requires union membership out of its employees. We have chosen to score states based on either a "yes" for the presence of a right-to-work law, or a "no" for the lack thereof. This information comes from the National Right to Work Legal Defense and Education Foundation, Inc.

TAX OR EXPENDITURE LIMIT

States were ranked by the number of state tax or expenditure limits in place. We measure this by i) a tax expenditure limit, ii) mandatory voter approval of tax increases, and iii) a supermajority requirement for tax increases. This information comes from the Cato Institute and other sources.

About the American Legislative Exchange Council

Founded in 1973, the American Legislative Exchange Council (ALEC) is the nation's largest, nonpartisan, individual membership association of state legislators, with 2,000 legislative members across the nation. ALEC's mission is to discuss, develop, and disseminate public policies, which expand free markets, promote economic growth, limit the size of government, and preserve individual liberty within its nine Task Forces.

CIVIL JUSTICE

To promote systematic fairness in the courts by discouraging frivolous lawsuits, to fairly balance judicial and legislative authority, to treat defendants and plaintiffs in a consistent manner, and to install transparency and accountability in the trial system.

COMMERCE, INSURANCE, AND ECONOMIC DEVELOPMENT

To enhance economic competitiveness, to promote employment and economic prosperity, to encourage innovation, and to limit government regulation imposed upon business.

ENERGY, ENVIRONMENT AND AGRICULTURE

To promote the mutually beneficial link between a robust economy and a healthy environment, and seeks to enhance the quality and use of our natural and agricultural resources for the benefit of human health and wellbeing.

EDUCATION

To promote excellence in the nation's educational system, to advance reforms through parental choice, to support efficiency, accountability, and transparency in all educational institutions, and to ensure America's youth are given the opportunity to succeed.

HEALTH AND HUMAN SERVICES

To reduce governmental involvement in health care, to support a consumer-driven health care system, and to promote free-market, pro-patient health care reforms at the state level.

INTERNATIONAL RELATIONS

To promote the core ALEC principles of free markets and limited government beyond our shores, to support final ratification of free trade agreements that create American jobs and grow our economy, and to protect the intellectual property rights of U.S. companies doing business overseas.

PUBLIC SAFETY AND ELECTIONS

To develop model policies that reduce crime and violence in our cities and neighborhoods, while also developing policies to ensure integrity and efficiency in our elections and systems of government.

TAX AND FISCAL POLICY

To reduce excessive government spending, to lower the overall tax burden, to enhance transparency of government operations, and to develop sound, free-market tax and fiscal policy.

TELECOMMUNICATIONS AND INFORMATION TECHNOLOGY

To advance consumer choice and deployment of new technologies in the dynamic and converging areas of telecommunications and information technology by furthering public policies that preserve free-market principles, promote competitive federalism, uphold deregulation efforts, and keep industries free from new burdensome regulations.